LA MIRADA

· A BRIEF HISTORY ·

RAYMOND FERNANDEZ AND GLEN CANTRELL

THE History PRESS

Published by The History Press
Charleston, SC
www.historypress.com

First published 2021

Manufactured in the United States

ISBN 9781467148382

Library of Congress Control Number: 2020948636

Notice: The information in this book is true and complete to the best of our knowledge. It is offered without guarantee on the part of the authors or The History Press. The authors and The History Press disclaim all liability in connection with the use of this book.

This book is dedicated to two determined ladies: Alice Palicz and Myllie Taylor. Both are treasures of La Mirada and acquaintances, known for their willingness in everything each ventured out to accomplish. Alice Palicz has many unforgettable qualities, other than being a self-starter. Myllie Taylor is known for her devotion and allegiance to the people she encounters and her consistent commitment to the history of La Mirada.

Also, this book is devoted to the city government as well as all of the residents of La Mirada past, present and future.

CONTENTS

ACKNOWLEDGEMENTS

I would like to first, and foremost thank God and my beautiful family, which includes my wife, Adriana; my son, Presley; and my daughter, Isabel Fernandez; Rudy, Sabrina and Andrew. I would like to thank the City of La Mirada and the La Mirada Historical Preservation Committee. Also, due thanks go to the La Mirada City Council, whose current and former members include Steve De Ruse, Ed Eng, John Lewis and Larry Mowles. I would also like to thank Lisa Montoya, who did a great job of being a conduit between the city, Glen and me. Also thanks to Jeff Boynton, city manager; the Sanchez family; my mother, Lupe Ballesteros; and my grandmother Eva and grandfather George Sanchez; Danny, Sylvia and Patty; the Pacheco family; my in-laws Norma, Jerry and Janae; as well as Dustin Engles, Tiana, Desiree and Geno Meza and Jerry Pacheco II. I would also like to acknowledge my father-in-law, Jerry Pacheco, and thank him for his service and his Purple Heart in the Vietnam War and a forty-two-year resident of La Mirada. Moreover, I want to express my appreciation of the small circle of trust friends, who gave me the fondest memories of growing up in La Mirada, California. I am much obliged to the Luis Garcia and family; the Ciceros, Frank and Lei, and family. Thank you Yair Wein, David and Marion Putt, Mike Stimler, Victoria Molina and certainly from the La Mirada High School days, as well as my Hutchinson Elementary School days and, naturally, the cook himself, Glen Cantrell and his daughter Elise Cantrell and his wife, Mary Cantrell. One supplementary name we do not want to pass over is our acquisitions editor, Laurie Krill. Laurie emailed me way back in June 2019 and we chatted online about an Arcadia/The History Press publication about the city of La Mirada. Laurie Krill waited patiently during the lengthy time it underwent. Thank you, Laurie, for being tolerant.

INTRODUCTION

You, dear readers, hold in your hands the fulfillment of the dreams of Raymond Fernandez and Glen Cantrell. These two passionate gentlemen grew up in La Mirada, and they wanted to share the city's rich history with everyone far and wide.

My name is Alice Palicz, and I arrived in La Mirada in 1953. I literally began working for the community during my first week for Lela Criswell, the postmaster at the depot, and then became the city's treasurer for many years.

Raymond and Glen met me first on their journey to put together this manuscript and sought out Myllie Taylor. Myllie is the historical guru. It was quite apparent that Raymond and Glen wanted La Mirada's fantastic history to be put down in print for succeeding generations.

Thus, this History Press book was born. I am very excited that this book covers six decades. You, the reader, will be delighted with all the eclectic history, and I know you'll enjoy the photographs. This is a book you can pick up and get pleasure from over and over again, each time realizing a new memory.

Raymond Fernandez graduated from La Mirada High School in 1993. He is an insurance sales manager. Along with his sales proclivity, he has brought his fond memories of living in La Mirada to this project. Raymond always has relevant questions for each city councilman or woman as well as the mayor, including La Mirada legends that are still around today. It was obvious to me that La Mirada is dear to his heart.

Glen Cantrell is a 1976 graduate of La Mirada High School. He is a published author of three novels: *The Résumé*, *Untypical* and *Reflections from McNally's Mirror*. Glen has tirelessly dug into the La Mirada archives and checked facts to bring clarity and background to the stories as well as acquired old photos with the permission of all of his sources. You have a big treat in store as you open these pages.

Each of the authors has poured his enthusiasm into this book. Perhaps as you read this, it will also trigger your own memories of La Mirada when you were growing up.

I have been a continuous La Mirada resident since 1953. We started the original *La Mirada Lamplighter* newspaper to hold the town together, and Dick Hurley corralled every significant story there was for years on years. Many people worked hard to create and preserve the worthiness of this city. May you enjoy every page as much as Raymond and Glen did as they saw this book to its conclusion. Thank you, Raymond Fernandez and Glen Cantrell.

Alice Palicz

PROLOGUE

The prologue is a chronological set of ten firsthand articles—stories and one poem starting as early as 1893. You'll note that the February 1904 story article is Andrew McNally's own story of how he became a ranchman in California, never before seen by any citizen of La Mirada. Andrew McNally is La Mirada's founder. McNally loved the land in which he selected. In 1890, he purchased 2,600 acres for their beauty and named this land La Mirada. He then started an enormous ranch and called it Windermere Ranch. In 1960, La Mirada became its own city. Also among these ten delightful time capsules is an article from 1905, which relates to how Edwin D. Neff, Andrew McNally's son-in-law, saved a total of $3,000 from one of God's saving insects known as the scutellista. Dear booklover, we'd like to bid you happy reading.

Boom in Olive Planting

Pacific Rural Press, *San Francisco, March 1896*

During the present planting season, large additions are being made to the olive acreage in many localities, and in the southern counties the movement has taken on the character of a boom. A Pomona letter reports that three groves, larger than any now in existence, are being planted in southern

California. The largest is that of Andrew McNally of the great publishing firm of Rand & McNally of Chicago. He has a gang of men at work laying out a 400-acre olive grove near Fullerton in Orange County. He will plant 40,000 olive trees.
Alfred Holman..........Editor
E.J. Wickson...........Special Contributor

AFTER A REST ON HIS OLIVE AND LEMON RANCH

San Francisco Call, *San Francisco, April 1896*

Andrew McNally, the great Publisher of Chicago, arrived here in San Francisco from Southern California yesterday, where he has been since November. Mr. McNally owns a magnificent residence at Altadena, and also a fine ranch of 2600 acres at La Mirada.

The ranch was purchased some five years ago, and is devoted to growing olives, lemons and barley. Mr. McNally estimates that in five years or more, the way his trees are thriving, he will produce 300 carloads of fruit a year.

He intends to make a specialty of marketing ripe and pickled olives. He is enthusiastic about California and the products of the trees and vines. He says he would rather plant a tree any day than take a big contract for printing.

THE WINDERMERE RANCH

The Republican Journal, *Belfast, Maine, March 1900*

The Los Angeles Times *of Jan. 26th gives the following description of one of the famous ranches of the Pacific Coast at La Mirada, California.*

The ranch is owned by Andrew McNally, the Chicago Publisher, and is located in the southeastern portion of Los Angeles County.

The Windermere Ranch contains 2600 acres, all in cultivation. It presents a combination of fruit, grain and stock interests that cannot fail to be edifying to those who have the opportunity of visiting the ranch. It is not every big ranch that can boast of a professional chemist, exclusively employed on the ranch, or that has a flour-making plant devoted only to grinding grain and feed for man and beast at home. So many novelties are in operation upon the Windermere ranch that a description of some of them must surely be of interest to the farmers of the country.

The ranch contains 51,000 trees in all. Of these 33,000 are olive, 16,000 lemon and 2,000 grape fruit. By average, the ranch has 800 in fruit trees, 1,400 in wheat, barley and corn, 40 in alfalfa, 40 in parks, 75 in pasturage, and the balance in yards, grounds, school, depot and laboratory sites. Many a small principality has had less value of investment than has been necessary to equip this big ranch.

In all, about 250,000 have been employed in purchasing, planting and equipping the ranch. Its cultivation alone requires the work of twenty men, forty-two mules and eight horses, used principally in orchard work, but sufficient to plant and harvest two square miles of grain. In the economy of ranch work here, the farm has its own artesian wells, flour mill, slaughter house, commissary, boarding house, blacksmith shop, paint and wood-working shops, laboratories for manufacturing two or three by-products from its fruits, lemon-curing house and dairy.

The stock department has about fifty hogs, Poland and Berkshire. The meat is all consumed on the ranch; fifty head of high-bred cows for the home dairy, of the Jersey and Holstein stock. There are well arranged and extensive sheds for hog-feeding, with the latest appliances for economical fattening. The cows are housed in modern sheds.

Nothing is wasted in the way of fertilizer anywhere about the place, and cement ditches and tanks are connected with the flow from an artesian well, so flushing can be done easily and thoroughly.

In the machinery department are found duplicate plows, rolling cutters, pulverizers, everything needed for cultivating the ranch, so that with the whole force at work on the farm and orchard, the blacksmith has a complete set of implements at hand for repairs—an economical arrangement of great value in rushing the work upon the farm. One large shed is devoted entirely to the storage of steam engines, sprinklers, sprayers, farm wagons and other vehicles, and to see the array of machines, implements, tools and appliances is to wonder at the magnitude of the equipment necessary for the running of a large California ranch.

The ranch-house of the Windermere is called the Neff House and it is a fine specimen of modified mission architecture and the depot building is of the same design, adding very much to the beauties of the big farm. Andrew McNally had this beautiful ranch home built for his daughter, Nannie. Her husband Edwin Neff is living there and assuming duties.

A small lake has been built near the residence of Mr. Neff, surrounded by a park, which will some-day be a great attraction, as it now is to an extent, through the planting of numerous varieties of ornamental trees and shrubs. The park contains over forty acres, and is near the depot.

In the orchards of this ranch, a perfect system of tree numbering is in use. The orchards are plotted. Every row is lettered to show the variety of fruit, and numbered for convenience in locating individual trees. Some of the orchard rows are more than a mile long.

The ranch is virtually self-sustaining. It produces its own wood, water, meats, breadstuffs, vegetables and fruits.

We look to the ranch at La Mirada for some valuable pointers upon olive growing also, and in the manufacture of oil and a new by-product the chemist of the farm hopes to produce.

A Remembrance of Andrew McNally—The Farm in Summer

Pacific Rural Press, *San Francisco 1900*

In all the world I do not know
A scene that stirs the wanderer so;
In all the world I have not found
A rarer joy, a holier ground
Than this, with all its wholesome charm—
The summer homestead and the farm.
Once more is ours the proud delight
To look upon the thrilling sight
Of nature's richest offerings,
Of fields astir with growing things.
The ample farms, afar and nigh,
Their songs of plenteousness reply,
And hillside acres, everywhere,
Echo the valleys, green and fair.
The fields the farmers might display,
For summer is his working day;
Whatever reaping days may bring,
To-day he is the summer's king.
----------*Country Gentleman*

OLIVE PRESSING UNDERWAY—CRUSHING OLIVES

Pacific Rural Press *and* California Fruit Bulletin, *San Francisco, 1902*

The new olive press at McNally's La Mirada Ranch is crushing ten tons a day and has made 5,000 gallons of oil. The ranch comprises 510 acres of olives, about one fourth in bearing. The question of picking has been a serious one, but McNally's son in law, Manager Edwin Dorland Neff has invented a scheme that reduces the cost to a minimum. He makes rakes by driving 12-penny nails through a cross-piece of wood, and has four men to the tree. They rake the fruit off, letting it fall on a two-piece sheet spread underneath. Cost of handling by this method is from $8 to $10 per ton.

THREE MOST CHARMING COUNTRY PLACES OF THIS SOUTHERN LAND

Los Angeles Herald, *Los Angeles, 1902*

It is a picturesque mission station, known as La Mirada. Eighteen miles south of Los Angeles on the Santa Fe Railroad built in the historic Spanish style with red tiled roof and a stone corridor. It lends a pleasing touch of color to the monotone of perfectly cultivated land surrounding it.

A short distance back of the station and extending in waving lines to the foothills is Andrew McNally's olive grove and adjoining this on the right is the "Rives Ranch."

On the left is the "Bob Northam home place," a beautiful piece of land consisting of eighty-six acres. A drive-way, banked on either side with a profusion of rare roses, leads to a park; where-in is a collection of trees and plants from different corners of the globe. Vines and flowers trail at will over the terrace where lately, Mr. Northam's home was destroyed by fire.

Palms, shrubs and ferns remain as in the old days, attesting to former magnificence and present beauty.

On this ranch, the soil of which is rich, sandy loam, we have fifty-five acres planted to soft shell walnuts, six-years-old in bearing along with naval and Valencia oranges; twenty-five in almonds, two acres in barley and one-half acre planted to deciduous fruits for home use.

All trees are in bearing and of the choicest varieties for irrigation. There is an abundance of artesian well water obtained from three wells varying in depth from 500 to 700 feet, each equipped with a steel windmill and pumping plant.

The water is stored in two large cement reservoirs from which it is carried throughout by means of underground pipes. This distributes the life giving fluid over every part of the land.

Finally, there's a large two-story house now being occupied by the caretaker and the caretaker's wife. The entire place is fenced. The ranch is in excellent condition and there is no more ideal spot for the home-seeker. An ardent of beauty this is in a land so fitted by nature for life in the country.

Andrew McNally tells how he became a ranchman in Southern California. *California Digital Newspaper Collection, Center for Bibliographic Studies and Research, University of California, Riverside.*

ANDREW MCNALLY TELLS HOW HE BECAME A RANCHMAN IN SOUTHERN CALIFORNIA

Los Angeles Herald, *Los Angeles, 1904*
By Andrew McNally, February 1904

When I spent my first winter in Southern California, in 1880–81, Los Angeles was a village, with unpaved streets and dirty and untidy hotels. Pasadena was a scattered settlement of small ranches. I shall always remember New Year's Day of 1881—my first in California. I lived at the Sierra Madre villa, on the foothills of the Sierra Madre Mountains, and about five miles from Pasadena. The day was bright, warm and genial; a cloudless sky of the deepest blue—such a sky as is seen only in semi-arid regions. Flowers, wild and cultivated, everywhere, which with the bloom of the orange and lemon trees, were as grateful to the sense of smell as the unrivaled scenic effects were to the eye. The mocking-bird, meadow-lark, linnet and many other varieties of song birds, added charm to this favored region. It seemed to me a mid-winter paradise, and "knowing a good thing when I saw it," I determined to own some of it.

After casting around in Southern California for several winters, visiting ranches on the coast and inland, I purchased the land (2600 acres) now known as the Windermere Ranch. It lies seven miles southeast of Los Angeles on the Santa Fe railroad, and about ten miles from the Pacific Ocean. Part of the ranch is rolling; part level mesa or tableland and part moist or low pasture land. There was no water on the land, nor a tree of any kind. Six artesian wells were sunk, about 600 feet deep, from four of which was obtained a good flow of water. The property cost $30 an acre. About 400 acres now have water for irrigation and are worth about $250 an acre without improvements.

In 1893, I started tree planting. First we planted a four-acre home orchard. The variety of trees in this orchard will give the reader an idea of the wide range of fruits, which can be grown in Southern California; oranges, lemons, limes, citron, pomelo (or grape fruit), fig, guava, nectarine, loquat, pomegranate, quince, cherry, apple, pear, peach, almond, apricot, walnut, pecan, many varieties of grape, including the hothouse varieties, blackberry, raspberry and other small fruits. It is a fact that from this orchard can be picked ripe fruit from the tree every day of the year.

During the three succeeding years were planted 500 acres of olive trees, 175 acres of lemon trees, forty acres of pomelo and shade trees, on about six miles of ranch roads. Some of these shade trees, all evergreen, have grown forty feet high in seven years, with trunks three feet in circumference. About 800 acres of the Windermere Ranch are planted to fruit trees, 1400 acres to grain, 300 acres to pasture and 100 to ornamental trees, lawns and roads, including Windermere Lake, which with the surrounding park, occupies thirty acres.

The olive, lemon and grape fruits are the principal fruits grown on the ranch. I have nearly 50,000 olive trees. Many varieties of olives have been imported from Europe to California, but the best and most reliable is the Mission olive, brought from Spain by the Jesuit Fathers, who established the California missions and planted the olives, with other fruit, 130 years ago. Many of these old olive trees are still growing today, hale and hearty, yielding good crops, showing that the bearing age of the olive tree seems to be unlimited.

Our lemon trees are "a thing of beauty and a joy forever." The lemon is the emblem of productiveness. At all seasons of the year can be found on the lemon tree the blossom, the tiny formed lemon, and lemons in all stages of growth to the full grown fruit. It is a perpetual bearer. The blossom, the leaf, the wood, the fruit, and all parts of the tree are delightfully fragrant.

I can imagine no more independent or pleasant life than that of a ranchman in California. He can work his ranch every day in the year, except from twenty to thirty days of rain, and he can pick and gather, every day of the year, fruit and vegetables for his table. With a few acres of alfalfa, he has perpetual pleasure with his stock, winter and summer. My ranch has been a source of pleasure and satisfaction to me, and it would be to anyone who has any degree of love for nature.

Coming from the bustle, noise, dust and smoke of a large city, the peaceful quiet and the beauty and fragrance of the orchards make one forget the strenuous battle of business life, and are a healthy and natural tonic, mentally and physically. To some men, not many I hope, a country life is tiresome.

With water for irrigation, the man of limited means can certainly obtain a larger income from forty acres in California than he can from eighty acres east of the Rocky Mountains. The last few years have not been so profitable for the citrus fruit growers, owing principally to the inability of the railroad companies to haul the fruit to market. I know orange ranches where the crop has been sold for over $1000 per acre, and lemon ranches are equally profitable.

The English walnut is a comparatively new industry and the trees are constant bearers. The crop of a 10-year-old grove will sell for upwards of

$200 per acre, while the cost of irrigation and cultivation will not exceed $10 per acre. The yield of a vineyard, either of table raisin or wine grapes sold at $15 a ton, which is a minimum price, will net at least $100 per acre. Grapes in California yield immense crops without irrigation. Raisin and table grapes are sometimes irrigated to produce larger grapes, but for wine, the fruit grown without irrigation is preferred.

Two years after planting, the trees begin to bear, and when well taken care of, a four-year-old lemon tree will yield two boxes of fruit. On the Windermere Ranch, a band of pickers are always at work, except during wet weather in the winter. The fruit is picked from the tree once a month. The full grown lemon should measure two and one-fourth inches in diameter. It is picked according to size, regardless of color, and is usually quite green when picked. It must be handled as carefully as eggs, as the slightest bruise will rupture the oil cells in the rind and cause rapid decay. The picker has a half-circle shaped basket, lined with flannel, strapped around his waist, to receive the fruit; in his right hand a strong scissor-like cutter with which he cuts the stem of the lemon close to the fruit.

Until within a few years, California imported nearly all the eggs, poultry, ham and bacon and potatoes used in the state. Even now a large proportion of these products are imported, while all can be raised in California at less cost than in the east.

Persons desiring homes in California, either for health, pleasure or profit, should spend considerable time in studying the conditions. A newcomer (or tenderfoot as the natives call him) is very liable to become enthusiastic over the beautiful climate and tropical appearance of the California winter. In this condition, he is apt to believe all the statements of the wily real estate agent and "buy in haste and repent at leisure."

For the invalid, the foothills with an elevation at from one thousand to two thousand feet above sea level, is preferable. Here, he will be free from the sea fogs, which are frequent in winter and summer on the coast, and he will find the air clear and bracing. A home for profit had better be selected in the valleys, where water can easily be obtained from wells. In growing citrus fruits, the foothills are generally preferred, but these are successfully grown on valley land.

To a man of means and leisure, Southern California presents many attractions. Good trout fishing can be had in the mountain streams, and the deep-sea fishing off Catalina Islands has a world-wide celebrity. Bear and deer can be found in the mountains. Quail are plentiful in the valleys and foothills.

SCUTELLISTA SAVES ORCHARDIST

Pacific Rural Press, *Agricultural Review, San Francisco, 1905*

$3000, Azusa, California: We enjoyed a short visit with Horticultural Commissioner J. W. Jeffrey Tuesday, and, in speaking of the scutellista and the wonderful work it is accomplishing he said; "Fifty cars of holiday fruit have been shipped to date from Whittier. The oranges were neither sprayed or fumigated and washing was unnecessary, owing to this industrious little insect. On the McNally Ranch, La Mirada, southeast of Los Angeles, one of the largest in southern California, the scutellista is estimated to have saved the owner in the neighborhood of $3000 this year."

MOST FAMOUS PLACES IN SOUTHERN CALIFORNIA

The Minneapolis Journal, *Minneapolis,* MN, *1905*

Eighteen miles from Los Angeles, California, 630 acres; on Santa Fe railway, adjacent to the towns of Buena Park, Fullerton and other prosperous settlements; also adjoining the lands of Andrew McNally of Rand, McNally & Co., La Mirada and George B. Reeve, formerly general manager of the Grand Trunk railway. These are the most famous places in Southern California. The rental income for grazing purposes last year from Edgebrook Ranch was $6,000.

MANURE SPREADERS NEED IMPROVEMENT

Pacific Rural Press, *San Francisco,* CA, *1920*

"We have worn out two manure spreaders and are now hauling with the third one," said Supt. R.C. McGill of the McNally Ranch in Los Angeles County recently in commenting on the satisfactory performance of the machines. Much finer and superior distribution of manure by the spreader in the citrus and olive orchards and greater economy of unloading are the advantages mentioned by Mr. McGill for manure spreaders.

Manure is hauled on this ranch for three seasons of the year. This fall about 600 tons are being supplied on the orchard from his own corrals and from those within hauling distance. Half of this is being hauled with the spreader, the rest being hauled by wagon because the spreader is not figured to be economical for more than a half-mile haul, and it could not haul more than 300 loads within the desired time.

The flatbed wagon carries twice as much as the spreader, but it requires three men, including the driver, to unload it economically and with coarser, poorer distribution than the machine gives. Two of these men are idle, going back and forth. The driver alone unloads as much from the spread as two men could from the wagon. It takes four horses to pull the wagon; and the same number to pull the spreader when the ground is soft. The amount hauled per day by the spreader depends on the distance and the rapidity of loading. With two spreaders working and one man constantly at the manure pile to help the driver load, the spreader hauled two loads per hour two seasons ago.

Commercial fertilizer, tankage, etc., are loaded onto a thin layer of manure in the machine and then distributed satisfactorily.

Why Dump Manure in Piles?

All over the country we have observed piles of manure dumped by motor trucks at the edges of orchards, there to heat and lose value until used, and to be expensively pitched onto wagons or spreaders later for distribution. "Why?" asked Mr. McGill, "do not the orchardists avoid that extra work by having the manure dumped on a platform whence it could be loaded into a spreader by gravity with a scraper through a chute?"

Engine Would Save Horses

An improvement desired by this rancher is a lower gear on the machine to save power pulling it in the orchard. Perhaps a better proposition would be a small engine hitched to dump the manure while horses merely haul it with no unloading gear attached to the wheels. This would eliminate two horses and would probably make it possible to use the spreader on softer or wetter land than where the beaters and apron are operated from the rear wheels.

PART I.

THE HISTORY

In 1890, a transaction occurred between Abel Stearns's Ranchos and Land Company and Andrew McNally that would alter the course of history for a section of land today referred to as La Mirada. *Courtesy of Gail Pearce from the La Mirada City Archives.*

1
THE BEGINNINGS AT THE TURN OF THE CENTURY

A History of La Mirada, California

Andrew McNally's Colony Plan and the Windermere Ranch

1890, 1905

La Mirada is today (2021) a suburb of Los Angeles that comprises the area between the city of Whittier on the northwest and the city of Buena Park on the southeast. This city, incorporated in 1960, lies near the Los Angeles County–Orange County boundary and northwest of Coyote Creek, being within Los Angeles County. In 1952, this area resembled the acreage that formed the Windermere Ranch in 1905. Although there were many acres of the original Windermere Ranch, which had been leased out to tenant farmers by 1952, the majority of the land had been left as it was when the Windermere Ranch was the world's largest olive oil producer.

As part of the Rancho Los Coyotes, La Mirada has a history that dates back nearly two hundred years. This rancho was part of a vast concession of 300,000 acres given in 1784 to Manuel Nieto by the Spanish governor Pedro Fages. This concession was again divided in 1834 by Governor José Figueroa, and the Rancho Los Coyotes, taking its name from the creek that bisected it, was granted to Juan José Nieto.

In 1890, Abel Stearns's Ranchos and Land Company bought Rancho Los Coyotes. That same year, a transaction occurred between Abel Stearns's

Ranchos and Land Company and Andrew McNally, a wealthy businessman from Chicago and Altadena, that was expected to alter the course of history for the section of land today referred to as La Mirada.

For years, the land had been used merely for the grazing of cattle and sheep, first as part of the Los Coyotes Rancho and later as a section of Abel Stearns's tremendous holdings in Los Angeles and Orange Counties. This area lacked a constant water supply, thus failing to attract serious ventures into farming.

Yet in 1890, two years after the Southern California Railway laid track from San Diego to Los Angeles through La Mirada, and three years after the great Land Boom of 1887 had broken, causing a depression in most parts of Southern California, Andrew McNally bought 2,600 acres of land just northwest of Los Coyotes Creek for an amount of $115,000. Although this sum, $50 per acre, was a high price to pay for the land at the time, Andrew McNally felt that the investment was safe.

Andrew McNally had been planning since 1879 to create, construct and promote a fantastic "colony of Country Gentlemen." The colony plan was not a new one, for it had been used several times, and, in fact, had its origin in Southern California.

McNally, however, visualized that his purchased land would become a colony of country estates, inhabited mostly by well-to-do gentlemen from the East. These estates would be in twenty- or forty-acre plots and would be planted mainly with either olive or lemon trees. These particular trees were chosen first because their yield was in great demand during the 1890s, and second because they were expected to grow very nicely in the environment of McNally's purchased land.

McNally realized that the gentlemen he was attempting to attract to his scheme would very likely not have the knowledge or the skills needed to plant and care for the olive and lemon trees during their early years, a critical period in their growth. For this reason, Andrew McNally presented a proposition that would eliminate the need for the country gentleman to live on his acreage for the first four years of his ownership. During these crucial years in the plants' growth, Andrew McNally's workers would care for the trees and nurse them to maturity. Then after four years, the orchard would be turned over to the owner.

Although there was no public notice of the price that Andrew McNally wanted for his twenty-acre plots, there is proof that he wanted to allow a man who had only a few thousand dollars to become a country gentleman and an agricultural success. For this reason, McNally tried to make the plan for the purchase of the land and its improvements as easy as possible. This arrangement asked the buyer to pay one-quarter at the time the contract was signed and one-quarter of the total price during each of the following three years. The price was to be payment for the land, the planting and care of the trees for four years and for shares in the water company. To this price, McNally would add 6 percent interest. McNally believed that this plan would be fair to all parties since it would ensure the proper management of the land until the final payment was made and the proper care for the orchards during the critical periods of growth.

In the colony, McNally planned to do more than merely be the seller and originator of the scheme. He planned to also be a country gentleman and landholder; he was to have seven hundred acres of his own land. He planned to build an olive oil factory, operate a citrus packinghouse and construct several roads lined with trees.

Immediately after the purchase of the land, Andrew McNally had a railway station built out of white stone. He called the land La Mirada because of the beautiful view of the rolling hills combined with the flat meadows everywhere. He would often say that each time he would gape in the distance, it was breathtaking. La Mirada, a Spanish name meaning "the glance" or "gaze." There would be other interpretations of the name La Mirada. The view, the look and the mirror would be three of those interpretations. He placed the name La Mirada on the front of his train station. The La Mirada station was the first step at developing the land after its purchase. This station was built in an old Spanish style so that it would match the other buildings on the ranch, such as the McNally olive oil factory, which would be built across the tract from the station at a later date. The railway station received its first station agent in 1892 in the person of A.E. Dressel who later lived on the second floor of this station and doubled as postmaster after 1903.

The trains stopped at the station twice a day to pick up passengers and leave the mail off; La Mirada was one of the main stops on the Southern California line.

In addition to constructing the railway station, Andrew McNally began drilling artesian wells in an effort to obtain water so that future colonization could occur. Although La Mirada suffered from a lack of water, McNally knew from the results of a series of water tests taken prior to his purchase of the land that there was an abundance of water below its surface. In the early 1890s, McNally began drilling for water and found there to be clear, pure water rated higher than most springs. It showed only 8.32 grains of

La Mirada Depot. *Wikimedia.*

solid matter per U.S. gallon, and each solid particle was either harmless or beneficial in its quantities. Pipelines were built to transport the artesian water from the wells to surrounding acreage so that the entire colony would receive an equal supply.

Immediately after the artesian wells were drilled, McNally began further developing La Mirada by planting orchards. The land was extremely fertile, as it had been used for the pasturing of sheep for many years, and capable of supporting almost any type of crop. McNally began planting lemon and olive trees in great numbers.

Lemon trees are evergreen, and generally, the foliage is rich green in color. These trees are constant bloomers, giving fruit year-round. This allows for one man to care for more plants than if harvest occurred only once a year. Also, lemons can be held for several months before being sent to market, thus allowing one to select when the best time was to sell. La Mirada in 1890, as today, had an ideal climate for the production of lemons, since the area rarely experienced frost. Also, the lemons enjoyed a fairly good price in the market and commanded a constant and steady demand.

The olive tree is also an evergreen. It has deep roots and requires very little water when matured; this enabled the growers to plant the olive tree on the high tablelands and on the slopes in La Mirada without worrying that the tree might die from an insufficient amount of water.

The olive oil processed from the olives was in great demand during the 1890s. This oil was primarily used for cooking oil but was also used in the packaging of sardines and as a soothing agent for burns as well as for wounds produced by friction and irritations of the skin. In addition, olive oil was used to anoint and soften babies' bodies. This product can be stored for an unlimited amount of time without fear of it spoiling.

In addition to olives and lemons, McNally planted several acres of alfalfa. This crop was mainly used to feed the work animals on the ranch, but there were positive plans for the marketing of this crop in the future.

In 1893, Nannie McNally, Andrew McNally's daughter, married Edwin D. Neff. Shortly after their marriage, the couple moved to La Mirada, where Edwin was to manage McNally's ranch. The home that they were to move into, which is now referred to as the Neff Home, was built soon after the wedding. It is believed that the house might have been built especially for the young couple. This building is a two-story structure of Spanish design.

In approximately 1896, Andrew McNally formed the La Mirada Land Company by transferring 1,500 acres of the original purchase of 1890 to the La Mirada Land Company to be used for the purpose of promoting the country gentlemen colony plan. The capital assets of the La Mirada Land Company were figured at $200,000 in 1896. The land held by the La Mirada Land Company was referred to interchangeably by the names Windermere Ranch and McNally Ranch, the latter applied mainly only to the commercial interests of the company. At the time of the incorporation of the La Mirada Land Company, Edwin D. Neff, McNally's new son-in-law, was appointed secretary and manager of the land company, while McNally became the president. The creation of this company is significant, since it was through this corporation that Andrew McNally planned to develop La Mirada into the colony of country gentlemen.

One of the first accomplishments made by the newly incorporated La Mirada Land Company was the publication of a promotional pamphlet titled *The Country Gentlemen in California*. This pamphlet was published in late 1896 and was designed for distribution in the eastern states. This pamphlet described Andrew McNally's colony plan and the advances that had been made to date. By the fall of 1896, 850 acres had been planted in lemon and olive orchards.

The Country Gentlemen in California described the Southern California climate as relatively constant year-round. California was referred to as the land of "continuous bright sunshine and soothing warmth" and an area unmolested by frost. The temperature in La Mirada normally varies from a summer average of 68 degrees to a winter average of 53 degrees. In the cold winter of 1895–96, the temperature did not go below 40 degrees Fahrenheit. This allowed the author of the pamphlet to write without stretching the truth. The climate made this area ideal for the production of citrus trees.

The Country Gentlemen in California contained many quotes from well-known figures of the day such as Chauncey Depew; famed railroad magnate Charles Dudley Warner, author of *The Italy of America*; and former California governor H.H. Markham. These writers described the paradise that was California and the profits that could be made from certain crops, such as olives and lemons. A letter from Markham was included, praising McNally on his venture.

The pamphlet also told of abundant game that could be hunted in the area surrounding La Mirada. There is a great amount of material today to support the fact that a large number of ducks and geese often frequented marshlands on the McNally property as well as rabbits and coyotes, which were also in plentiful supply in the Coyote Hills just east of the McNally Ranch.

In the pamphlet, the La Mirada Land Company also revealed its plans for the development of broad gravel roads to run through the colony. Trees lining these roads were to be of good quality and chosen with taste. By 1901, when Edwin D. Neff and his family left La Mirada, Andrew McNally had planted ten miles of ornamental trees in the colony. The roads were to run in a north–south direction and were named as follows: Olive Avenue (present-day Valley View Avenue), Windermere Avenue to pass the Neff residence, Cypress Avenue, Acacia Avenue, Araucaria Avenue (later changed to Luitwieler Avenue and more recently La Mirada Boulevard) and La Habra Avenue. Those roads running in an east–west direction were named La Mirada Avenue (later called Excelsior Avenue), Mesa Avenue, Rubra Street and Columella Street. Although these roads were, according to the pamphlet, considered excellent in 1896, they were not improved in later years and merely became dirt paths.

The development of a lake called Windermere was mentioned in the pamphlet. This lake was to be filled with fish, such as bass, and have aquatic plants grown in the shallow water near the shore. Rare trees and shrubs were to be imported so that a park could be constructed on the shore of the lake. This lake became a reality in the late 1890s and early 1900s, having been created northeast of the Neff residence between Windermere and Cypress Avenues. The lake, however, ceased to be cared for and was left to dry up.

In addition, the La Mirada Land Company revealed plans to erect two industrial plants, one for the processing of olive oil and the other for packing

La Mirada Depot looking north at the front of Andrew McNally's Windermere Ranch, 1904. *Courtesy of Gail Pearce from the La Mirada City Archives.*

citrus fruits. These plants were to be built for the interests of the whole colony. The McNally olive oil processing plant was built in 1897 across the Southern California Railway tracks from the La Mirada station. The citrus packing plant also became a reality and was constructed at a later date next to the olive oil plant.

The Country Gentlemen in California was published with the intention of attracting from forty-five to sixty upper-middle-class businessmen to the La Mirada colony. McNally tried to anticipate and provide for all their needs, but the ideal colony of country gentlemen failed to meet its goals. At Edwin D. Neff's departure in1901, Robert McGill, who had previously been a superintendent and the accountant for the McNally Ranch, became the manager for the La Mirada Land Company. At this time, he moved from his house, later called the George Home, into the Neff Home. Robert McGill did not abandon the colony plan until Andrew McNally's death in Altadena, California, on May 7, 1904, from pneumonia. At this time, however, the colony plan was shelved.

Under Robert McGill's management, the McNally Ranch became the largest olive orchard in the world, producing 15 percent of California's olive oil supply and having a total value of $4.5 million. The McNally olive oil factory on Stage Road across from the La Mirada railway station produced, at one point in time, the world's highest-quality olive oil.

La Mirada, California, circa 1904. The view is looking out of the sphinx entrance leaving the McNally Ranch headquarters. *Paul Burton collection.*

At the Windermere Ranch's peak production, it had six hundred acres planted with olive trees, two hundred acres of lemon trees and many more acres dedicated to alfalfa, grapefruit and oranges. To keep the ranch operating, the La Mirada Land Company needed a great number of workers. Some of the workers brought their families with them, and La Mirada grew to a population of approximately two hundred by 1897.

Andrew McNally was a nature lover and expected his employees and neighbors also to appreciate nature. He would import rare and beautiful songbirds, making a specialty of golden pheasants. He would help the birds adjust to the environment and then turn them loose. Almost every building constructed on the Windermere ranch was done at McNally's expense. Clustered around the manager's residence, today's Neff Home, were a barn, a stable, a mess hall for the ranch hands and a blacksmith shop. McNally also had houses built for the superintendents and administrators on the ranch.

A Japanese village was also built for McNally's Japanese employees and had an assembly room for them, a garden and individual rooms for the families. Although the Japanese workers lived in close quarters, they did not appear to be dissatisfied.

The county schoolhouse, which McNally had built, was a three-room affair with a belfry, two schoolrooms and a library. This school was located on the

McNally's olive oil plant, built in 1898. *Courtesy of Gail Pearce from the La Mirada City Archives.*

This is La Mirada's first school, erected in 1910 on the Windermere Ranch. The students are the ranch workers' sons and daughters. *Courtesy of Gail Pearce from the La Mirada City Archives.*

then La Mirada Avenue, later called Excelsior Drive. One schoolroom was for the first through fourth grades, and the other housed the fifth through the eighth grades. The school was used for the first time in approximately 1897, and the first teacher was a Miss L. McLain. The teachers were hired by the Los Angeles County School Board. They were usually young, unmarried women who would stay for one or two years at a time. Few of the teachers would live on the McNally Ranch. Several lived in Norwalk or commuted from Los Angeles each day on the train. Louis Blatz, who was a chemist for the McNally Ranch from 1897 on, served as a school board member for most of his life while in La Mirada.

La Mirada was about fifteen miles by train from Los Angeles and five miles from Fullerton, which was the nearest banking town, and three miles each from the two nearest towns of Buena Park and Norwalk. The ranch hands, however, did not frequent the surrounding towns during the week but stayed on the ranch. The work on the ranch would begin at six o'clock each morning, and all the heavy work, such as cultivating, was assisted by six-mule teams. The ranch workers were Mexican, American and Japanese. There is evidence that the American and Mexican workers were sometimes unhappy and dissatisfied with their conditions, but the Japanese workers were very orderly and well organized and were seldom caught complaining or quarreling among themselves. When more workers were needed, such as at harvest time, the ranch would contact the Los Angeles Employment Agency for the additional help.

The only transportation during this period, besides the train, was the horse and buggy. Buggies were used to and from the train station for inspection trips around the farm and by the children to get back and forth from school. There were very few occasions for a celebration on the part of the workers. Life on the Windermere Ranch was very simple.

On a few occasions, such as the Fourth of July, the ranch hands would celebrate by cutting watermelons and sitting in the shade of the pepper trees. There were also special occasions, such as the baptismal celebrations when the ranch hands would join their foremen and other administrators in food and dancing in the yard. Also, on at least one occasion, Andrew McNally imported an entire group of geishas directly from Japan to entertain his Japanese field hands.

2
NEFF PARK

La Mirada, a bit of the land rolling gently from the Sierra Madre Mountains to the sea, was once part of the vast Mexican land grant Rancho Los Coyotes. For decades, it remained pastureland, first for the long-horned, lean and tough rancho cattle, and later, after the droughts of the 1860s, sheep wandered along its hillsides and through the little meadows of the streams. Springtime brought forth lush growth of wild oats to nourish the sheep as well as the quail and the rabbit. Coyotes loped across the fields, and an occasional silhouetted figure of a horse and rider moved along the skyline.

Perhaps it was the serene beauty of this land backed by the distant peaks that attracted a man with a thought, a plan for a land colonized by small country estates.

Terms offered were one-quarter down, balance in equal payments over the next three years, such prices including the planting and care of the trees until the new owner assumed ownership upon completion of the contract. The remaining seven-hundred-acre parcel was devoted to McNally's personal investment and named Windermere Ranch after an ancestor's home in Scotland.

Andrew McNally, born of a Scots father and a Hollander mother, was the eighth child and was early forced to seek his own livelihood. Receiving his education in the common schools, he was apprenticed to learn the trade of a printer. Continuing the work after he had mastered the details, he rose from the humble youth to become a partner in the widely known

These are the horses of the McNally Ranch employees, 1890s. *Courtesy of the La Mirada Carriage Barn Archives.*

Rand, McNally and Company, master printer of atlases and globes used throughout the world.

He was a man of versatile ability and throughout his life left no effort uncompleted in broadening his own life and character as well as those who surrounded him. Home life was perhaps his greatest enjoyment. In Chicago, he acquired several residences, which he beautified in every possible way. When ill fortune struck, the disastrous Chicago fire of 1871, all his homes were burned out. He turned briefly to farming by purchasing an eighty-acre farm near Elmhurst, Illinois. However, Chicago was his home, and he returned there to rebuild, erecting five stone-front homes on the fashionable Park Avenue, opposite Lincoln Park. Once he reserved as his own Chicago residence, the others were given as gifts to his married sons and daughters. His wife, known before their marriage as Adelia M. Highland, was a native of Chicago and of a prominent family. She gave him four children: Frederick G.; Helen B. (Bedford); Nannie M., wife of Edwin D. Neff; and Elizabeth B. (Clow).

Andrew McNally purchased four hundred acres near Pasadena, California, in what is now Altadena, of his own naming. Here he developed

Orange crate art, 1910. A beauty's hand draws the curtain to reveal McNally's dream ranch. *Courtesy of Gail Pearce from the La Mirada City Archives.*

a paradise, surrounding his home with rare trees and shrubs obtained from tropical climates. His conservatory was a place of beauty. He bought rare plants and rare birds. Other easterners, all of financial means, observing the results of McNally's efforts, purchased individual parcels of the original four hundred acres. As they constructed elaborate homes, Altadena soon became famed for its residential beauty. McNally's entrance into the La Mirada colony plan was to be of a similar venture.

He had a deep interest in the communities of his homes and gave freely of his time in all progressive and enterprising movements. As chairman of the finance committee of the 1903 Chicago World Fair, he had considerable influence in the raising of $10 million among the merchants of Chicago. Retiring from the Rand, McNally and Company in 1896, he devoted his remaining years between his Altadena home, Chicago and La Mirada, where

Joy Brand, circa 1910s. Orange crate highlighting Andrew McNally's Windermere Ranch. *Courtesy of Gail Pearce from the La Mirada City Archives.*

a landscaped spur track along the main line near the station was reserved for his private coach. McNally's olive processing plant and citrus packing plant stood for many years as historical landmarks, the packinghouse being destroyed by fire in the 1930s, the olive processing plant destroyed by the Long Beach earthquake in 1933. The old historical railroad station, built in 1890, was leveled in 1962.

In 1940, the Neff family returned to La Mirada. William N. Neff, the fourth child of Edwin D. Neff and the grandson of Andrew McNally, assumed management of Windermere Ranch following Robert McGill's death in 1939. Robert McGill had been fondly referred to as the "Czar of La Mirada," as he was active in local politics and other matters affecting the general community of La Mirada. Neff, "Bill" to his many friends and associates, was born in Pasadena in 1904 and received his early schooling in Germany.

After returning to Pasadena, he became active in Scouting, receiving the distinction of being the first Eagle Scout to be awarded the pin in Pasadena. He attended Loyola High School in Los Angeles and then graduated from UCLA. In 1926, he married his childhood sweetheart, Mina, daughter of

Arthur Braly of Los Angeles. Until assuming the supervision of the McNally Ranch and moving into the ancestral home in La Mirada, Bill Neff had been associated with his brother Andrew in the pottery business.

Although leading a busy life in the management of the ranch, Bill Neff found time for other activities as a director in the Kings County Development Company in California. Neff was an officer in the Orange County Navy League and a member of the California Club of Los Angeles. He was also an accomplished photographer and skier and was one of the founders of the Southwest Ski Club of Los Angeles.

Active as a sportsman, he was also an avid nature lover like his grandfather Andrew McNally, an interest shared equally by Mina. He stocked the yard of the ranch home with many chickens, ducks and geese, along with encouraging wild birds to nest in the tree-covered area of the home. With the help of Jack George, he constructed dams on La Mirada Creek, forming

A beautiful orange crate, 1910. Windermere brand. *Courtesy of Gail Pearce from the La Mirada City Archives.*

nesting ponds for migrating fowl. The site of these ponds is now the Biola College Athletic field.

The nucleus of Neff Park originated in 1955, when Bill Neff leased to the Southeast Recreation and Park District, on a dollar a year and maintenance basis, three acres on the south and west sides of the Neff Home. Opened to the public in April 1957, Neff Park, La Mirada's first, was enjoyed by more than thirty thousand visitors up to March 1962, when it was formally dedicated to the park district by Bill and Mina Neff.

Bill Neff did not live to see the fulfillment of the old home area becoming the recreation and community center it now is, succumbing to a heart attack in his sleep during the early hours of the morning of April 24, 1962. Carrying out their mutual wishes, Mina Neff sold eight acres that included the old carriage barn (Neff Barn) and the George Home to the park district in 1963. Later, she donated the remaining two acres, including the historical old home to the park district, thus completing the ten-acre compound for development into a public recreation and culture center.

Welcome to the Neff Home

Andrew McNally envisioned the eastern acreage as a colony of country gentlemen's homes. His vision was not fulfilled until the mid-1950s. This deters not one bit from the rich heritage of La Mirada.

Following are the lives of the families who once resided here. First was the Edwin D. Neff family (1894–1902), then the Robert McGill family (1902–1940) and Bill and Mina Neff 1940–1962, who were instrumental in preserving this home and the other buildings as part of the ten-acre Neff Park.

The George Home and Windermere Ranch

Known as the superintendents' cottage at the beginning of the Windermere Ranch, it became the foreman's home after Manager Robert McGill moved into the Neff Home in 1903. The Jack George family lived here for fifty years. Jack George, first employed by the ranch in 1910, returned to his native England in 1913 to marry and bring back his bride, Anne. After he

A recent photo of McNally's Windermere Ranch headquarters, the Neff Home. *Wikimedia.*

became foreman in 1914, he and Anne moved into the home where their two daughters, Marguerite and Daphne, were born. The family continued to live in the old home until 1964. Jack died in 1960, and Anne and her daughters, still at home, moved to one of La Mirada's modern homes.

The home is of quiet Victorian styling without a clutter of gingerbread trimmings. It represents houses popular as farm and urban dwellings during the late 1800s and early 1900s. Electricity and plumbing, installed after the house's construction, leads upward on the outside walls. The parlor fireplace chimney was removed following severe damage from the 1933 earthquake. The front door opens onto an entrance hall where a stairway reaches up to the second floor. The George Home is in the Neff Park compound at the entrance.

3

ROBERT McGILL, ALSO KNOWN AS R.C. McGILL AND THE "CZAR OF LA MIRADA"

Just prior to E.D. Neff leaving La Mirada in 1901, Robert McGill, then head accountant for the firm, was appointed manager of Windermere Ranch. The McGills' first home was in one of the company's houses on Excelsior Drive, later in the George Home. With his appointment as manager or superintendent of McNally's Ranch, the McGill family moved into the large home, now preserved as the Neff Home in present-day Neff Park.

Here they resided for nearly forty years. Two children were born prior to 1909, Margy and Robert Jr., and three other children—Grace, Mary (Mrs. William Badt) and Jean (Jean Raeder)—were born in the downstairs bedroom of the Neff Home. It had been converted from the library to the guest room and was fondly called the Baby Room by all the family.

In 1911, McGill hired Englishman Jack George as a teamster and later promoted him to ranch foreman. From 1914 until his death in 1960, Jack George lived with his wife and children in the home now preserved as the George Home also in Neff Park.

The ranch flourished during Robert "R.C." McGill's forty-year management, not only in the high quality of olive oil and the citrus fruit but also as a social center of the community.

Their home, the Neff house, was the scene of Red Cross benefits during World War I. Spirited dancing and singing occurred on the tennis court located in the rear of the house; the piano was laboriously carried out from the house.

Robert McGill and his family, circa 1920. *Bob Camp collection.*

Interest in these benefits was kept alive by the arrival of the Jenny planes, which used the land to the east as an emergency landing field whenever trouble developed on routine training flights between Los Angeles and San Diego. The field used as the landing was part of the only lengthy flat land in La Mirada, which became the La Mirada's Shopping Center.

McGill, called the "Czar of La Mirada" by the Norwalk newspaper during the high school district controversy, has been described by some as a strict taskmaster in his able management of the ranch. This is to his credit, as he was tutored in the nineteenth-century school of accountants; his zeal for detail is quite understandable. The responsibility of the ranch and the welfare of the workers living on the ranch rested heavily upon him, and his strictness was an honest fulfillment of both. He did not, indeed, coddle troublemakers amid the workers; he expected them to work and live with respect for the rights of others.

His seldom voicing of a greeting to the workers was not an intended slight; his personal goodwill toward them was well presented through the foreman, Jack George. One must consider that from the beginning, workers had been imported from countries when the feudal system was still recognized; the

La Mirada, California, pitted ripe olives select, 1949. *Alice Palicz collection.*

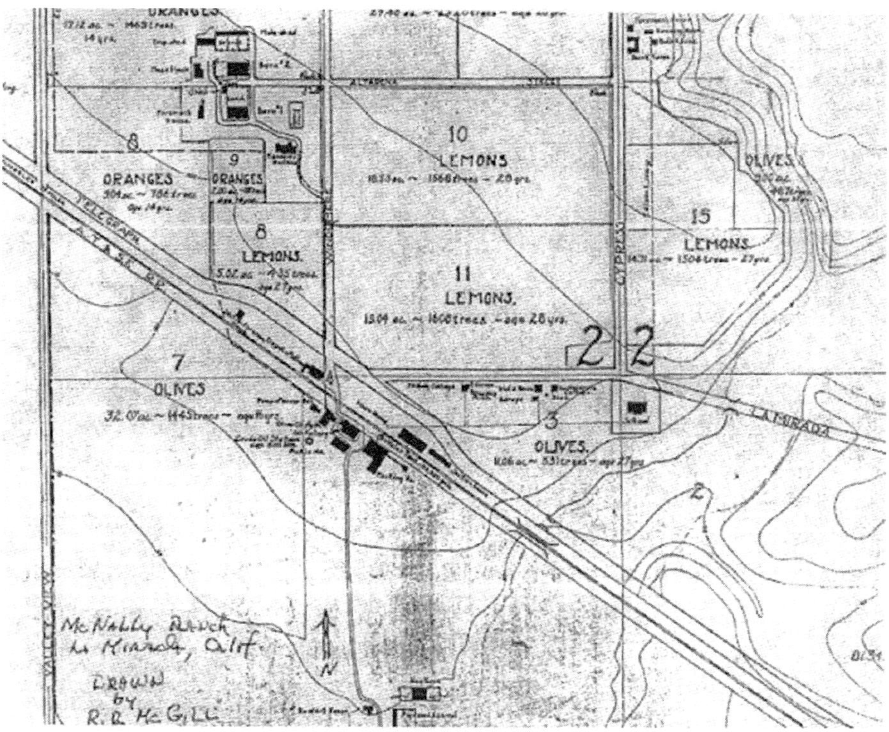

Hand-drawn map by Robert R. McGill. McNally's ranch manager from 1909 to 1939. Outlined in 1920. *Courtesy of Gail Pearce from the La Mirada City Archives.*

employees simply expected a continuation of the system at their new home and place of employment. There is no record of any serious dissent, and in these later years, many of the employees look back on their life on the ranch as good days.

Perhaps Robert McGill was the type of person Andrew McNally had in mind when he planned his colony. In an eastern state, he would have been considered a "country squire" of the nineteenth-century era, and indeed he did represent the distinguished country gentleman of that era, an era that came to a close with his death on April 29, 1940. R.C. McGill died on one of the lonely ranch roads during his attempt to free his car from a sand rut.

4

CITY OF LA MIRADA HISTORICAL COMMITTEE PRESS RELEASES 1966

Historically, research has revealed no record of the exact meaning of La Mirada, as applied. In discussing the name with the Mexican Consul Office in Los Angeles, we discovered an important factor. While the proper translation is "the look," with "gaze" or "glance" as acceptable variants, it would never be used as such by itself. And herein lies the key, La Mirada in Spanish would be used as the look, the gaze, the glance, the view at something whether it be the view, the mirror-like lake, the green orchards or toward the fulfillment of a dream. Pursuing this interpretation further, with the consideration of the Anglo-American habit of selecting one beautiful-sounding name or word from a descriptive Spanish phrase and using this as a place name, we can safely return to our legends. Perhaps La Mirada should remain as a symbol of a man's view, any man's, of his community.

La Mirada, pronounced properly, has a beautiful sound—need we search further?

La Mirada Was a Movie Location

Prior to 1952, the byway motorist briefly passed through a different realm as he drove along Stage Road. Here the tree-shaded sphinx guarded the ranch entrance and the railroad station and olive processing building represented a community untouched by the swiftly changing landscapes of the rest of the area. Some considered the community beautifully quaint, others as a bit of old-world atmosphere.

Hollywood moviemakers had already discovered this photogenic scene. Views were taken of the area to be catalogued for insertion in future movies. The sphinx could understandably be guarding the entrance to the headquarters of international intrigue or leading into a mansion of mystery. And, as shot from different angles, the station and olive factory could easily be included in any film of a Latin background. Who knows, perhaps the viewers of the late, late shows might see once again scenes of La Mirada as it was once.

And movies were actually filmed here, although these dealt not with the scenic view but with the slapstick comedies of the early silent films. The George sisters, Marguerite Courson and Daphne Meiers, recalled as mere tots watching the making of the Andy Gump comedies. These were a series of one- and two-reelers of the pie-throwing silent era with scenes of Andy Gump in such predicaments as getting dunked into a water tank. Anna George also recalled other comedies and location shots of films being made at the railroad station, site of the Andy Gump movies. Seats were furnished for spectators, who were entertained with all the behind-the-scene doings of a movie being filmed on location.

Trinidad Villegas

Behind the buffering walls of olive and lemon groves, the dwellers on the McNally Ranch lived almost in a separate domain. Families resided here, happily, in a pleasant rural atmosphere, and when they retired to their homes at nightfall, very little of the outside world intruded, except for the drifting mournful wail of train whistles speeding along Stage Road.

Trini, as Trinidad Villegas was known, arrived in La Mirada in 1926. In 1930, he and Arista Villefana were married and moved into the old bunkhouse located just north of the George Home in present-day Neff Park.

To the young bride, the bunkhouse, unused for many years, was a scary place. They had no need of the upper floor, and she never went up those stairs to what had been the bedrooms. Sounds issued from up there, the creaking of boards, occasionally an unexplainable moan like the last painful breath of a departing soul. Arista wasn't superstitious, yet she recalled old folktales heard as a child. And there were the ever-present owls, the weird monkey-faced owls whose hissing screams were heard during the night. Many of the old folk tales told of these owls being a part of witchcraft. It was a bad omen if one flew over a house. When the packinghouse foreman cottage became available near the present site of Rosecrans and Biola, the Villegas family moved from the old bunkhouse, and Arista was most happy.

The ranch was an idealistic spot to raise their five children, with fields to roam, the dark olive groves to explore and crawfish to catch in the muddy water of Lake Windermere. Animal life was abundant; watercress grew in the swampy ground near present-day Biola College. The ever-present subdivision was closing in on the Villegas; they were the last to leave. It was in 1955 when their home was leveled by the bulldozers.

Olive trees were planted in everyone's front yard starting in 1953. *Courtesy of Dick Hurley, editor in chief of the* La Mirada Lamplighter.

La Mirada? Ah, that was a happy home. What man could want more? But over the years we had times of violence, like the big gun fight in the early 1930s. Not a Hollywood version, no bad guys, no heroes, just a typical western shoot-out.

It all started during lemon pruning time. Now maybe there was a personal grudge mixed up with it, anyway, an argument started. Sides were taken, and then harsh words and threats. Before you knew it, several took off for their guns. It was sort of a stalking fight with 22's and big 45's, but it was soon over and everyone made up. Fortunately no one was hurt, unless you consider the action taken by manager Robert McGill. He quickly set his aim and did some "firing" of his own.

And there was the time one of the workers of the Blue Hills farms who hanged himself in the olive grove. No one knew why. Another time a trussed-up corpse was found, and again no-one knew why. Some say it was a hari-kari affair, although no one could figure out how he tied himself up. The deputies who searched the groves determined that the man had been killed elsewhere and his body brought into the dark grove.

And of course there was considerable excitement when the airplane crashed in the field south of the Olive Lawn Cemetery near Luitwieler Avenue. Officials were everywhere while the workmen removed the wreckage and smoothed over the scars to the earth.

But he who lived on the ranch remembered mostly the happy life. It was a good life, a simple life. Not too much of the hustle-bustle of social parties. Yes, it was a good life. When the day's work was over, after supper, one could sit outside under the sky and listen to the night sound of nature.

—as told to historian Bob Camp

Left: Dr. Sam Sutherland (*far left*), senior president of the Los Angeles location of Biola College, studies a raised model on how his La Mirada campus will look, 1957. *Courtesy of Loren Penner from Discover La Mirada.*

Below: La Mirada, California, 1957. Welcome to America's Most Completely Planned City. *Courtesy of Loren Penner from Discover La Mirada.*

5
LA POMELO RANCH

La Pomelo Ranch, a Showplace Retreat in Old La Mirada

In 1892, George Bell Reeve, a Canadian railroad executive, built his elaborate thirteen-room house on the site of today's Windermere Park. The ranch, one quarter section in the northeast corner of Alondra and Escalona, was also part of the area of La Mirada's first town site, the ill-fated Savanna of 1869.

Designed for gracious entertaining, the two-story house was surrounded by a circular driveway, and one can readily envision carriages arriving at the wide front door, which opened onto a large entry hall. Inside, to the left was a spacious parlor enhanced by a black marble fireplace with carved wood and a mirrored mantel. The dining room was adjacent, the butler pantry and the kitchen to the rear.

Often, after a formal family dinner, the women and the children would gather in the parlor for singing and music while the menfolk retired across the hall to the library or billiards rooms for discussion or pool games.

From the entry hall, the carved banister of the winding stairway led to the upper hall with the various bedrooms and the bathrooms on each side. Front rooms with large bay windows looked down on the five-acre garden of tropical plantings and an aviary of exotic birds. Gas for the houselights was generated from carbide, coal used for central heating by the furnace in the basement.

Rabbit and coyote hunting was quite the sport; Coyote Hills always furnished good shooting. The younger set engaged in lively tennis matches, often in spirited competition with the McGill children from the McNally Ranch.

The La Pomelo Ranch home was razed in 1955, and in 1957, the Southeast Recreation and Park District completed negotiations for the purchase of approximately four acres of its site for use as Windermere Park.

6
SUBDIVISIONS

Subdivisions 1953–1960

La Mirada Tracts of Homes

While what is generally considered the present La Mirada developed from the McNally Ranch, the first homes in the area, other than the ranch residences, were started in the late 1940s on a portion of the Autry Mayes Ranch (formerly the Reeve Ranch). Here, large lots were subdivided for custom homes for individuals who had been intrigued by the quiet rural life of the La Mirada area. Later, when the sale of the McNally Ranch was negotiated, the first housing tract still was not on McNally property.

Harold L. Shaw, purchaser of McNally Ranch, started his developments on Alondra Boulevard east of the Stage Road junction. Here Shaw purchased the triangular plot between Alondra and Stage Road from the McComber Ranch and on the north side of Alondra from the Mayes Ranch. This tract was known simply as Shaw No. 1 again in the late 1940s. Oddly, Shaw did not follow the established sales promotion procedure of naming tracts with colorful titles. All of his tracts were advertised as Shaw No. 1 and Shaw No. 2 only. Shaw No. 1 did, later, become known somewhat as La Mirada Highlands, a name suggested by Autrey Mayes; he had renamed his ranch the Highlands in the 1940s.

Harold L. Shaw's role as sole owner and developer of La Mirada was short-lived. In August 1954, Louis M. Halper, a prominent Southern California residential and commercial builder for thirty-five years, took over twenty-one thousand acres and formed the La Mirada Development Company. The reputed sale price of $8 million represented a huge increase in the value of the La Mirada area in the short span of two years. Halper's company was to be a guiding director by forming a new pattern in community building through wholesaling land to other developers of residential and commercial properties. He also established the La Mirada Civic Center where city hall and the library would be placed. In a period of twelve months, he set one of the best records for the sale of homes in the national building industry. Under his directorship, with a goal of ten thousand homes in two years, the development of La Mirada moved swiftly. By August 1956, thirteen tracts had been built and mostly sold.

With Shaw No. 1 completed and sold, the second area started was on Valley View south of Rosecrans. The tract, known as Parkwood La Mirada, was followed shortly by Harold Shaw's Shaw No. 2, just north of Rosecrans on Valley View. Shaw was now back in business constructing homes on land purchased from the Halper concern. Shaw next built his Shaw Master No. 1 on Alondra east of his first endeavor. In order, the following tracts were developed by August 1956: La Mirada Woods, Alondra and Escalona; Parkwood Terrace, near Biola and Rosecrans; Mesa La Mirada and Lucky Strike, Rosecrans and near Adelfa; Shaw Master No. 2, Rosecrans near Valley View; Parkwood Vista, north of Shaw No. 2 on Valley View; Crestview, near Santa Gertrudes, north of Rosecrans; Midland La Mirada, northeast corner of Luitwieler and Rosecrans; Parkwood Royale, Tacuba Drive south of Imperial; Shaw Master No. 3, on Biola near Biola College.

Until late 1955, Rosecrans did not extend beyond the confines of the La Mirada Creek, at which time the bridge was complete. In October 1956, funds were approved for a four-lane bridge over the Los Coyotes Creek, and with its completion in late 1958, Rosecrans Avenue opened up an important link with La Habra Road and made Rosecrans a continuous cross-country highway from the Pacific Ocean at Manhattan Beach eastward to the Orange County line at La Habra Road, now Beach Boulevard or Route No. 39.

Luitwieler Avenue, originally dead-ended at its intersection with Alondra, was linked with Beach Boulevard in January 1958 and is an important link between Imperial Highway and Buena Park. The mile-long, eighty-five-foot-wide extension lies in Orange County, and construction costs were worked out with that county.

By mid-1955, after just one year of growth under the direction of Halper and the La Mirada Development Company, 7,800 homes had been built, started or were ready to start, and 1,500 families were living in La Mirada.

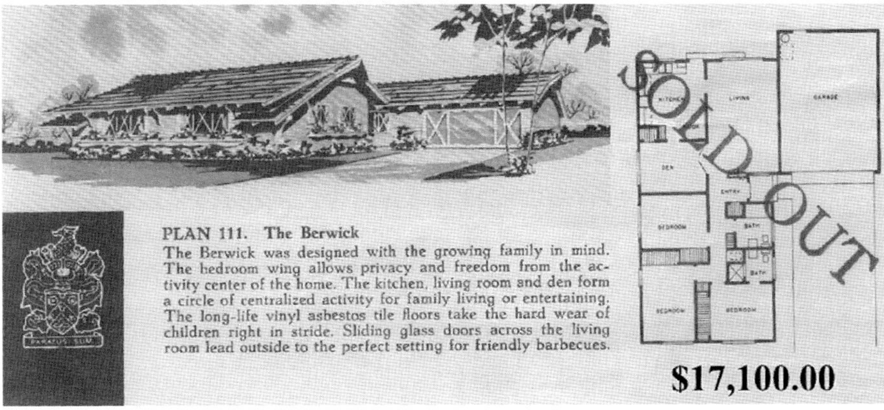

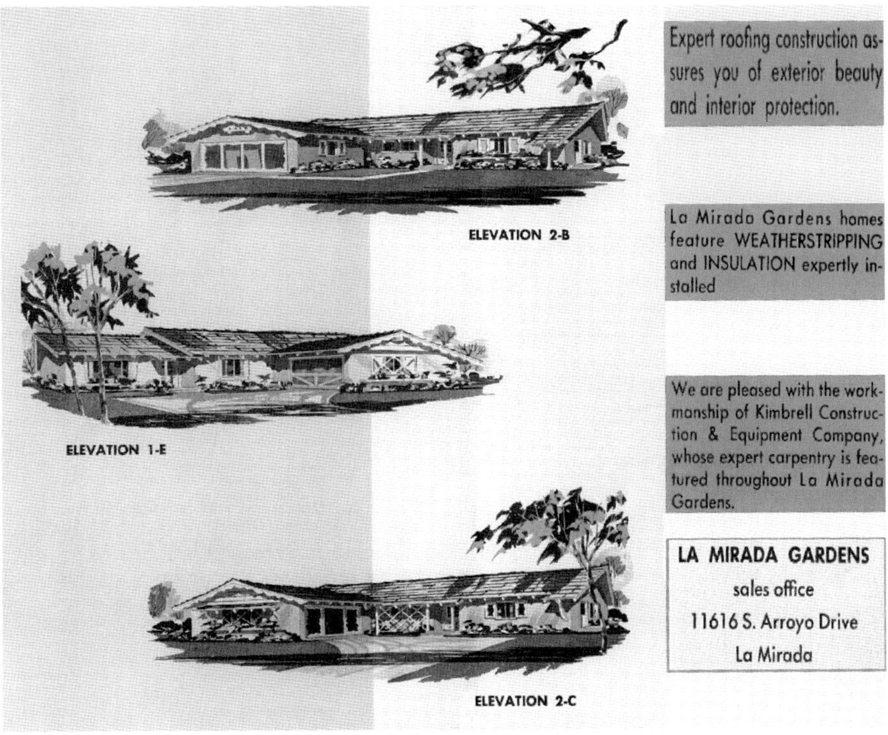

Top: These La Mirada residential dwellings became available in 1957. Publicized here is the Highland Glen Estates tract of homes. *Rand Cantrell collection.*

Bottom: A 1958 brochure from Kimbrell Construction & Equipment Company. This majestic tract is called La Mirada Gardens. *Courtesy of Gail Pearce from the La Mirada City Archives.*

7

POPULATION, PARKS AND RECREATION, CULTURAL ACTIVITIES, COMMERCIAL DEVELOPMENT AND EDUCATION

At the time of incorporation in 1960, La Mirada had a population of approximately twenty-three thousand within the city limits. This number would grow by means of new housing developments, which attracted new residents, annexation of existing residential development to the city and the presence of young growing families in the community. Proud of their new city, there was a machination. City leaders and residents wanted the old La Mirada name back. Both La Mirada Knolls and Mirada Hills had been chosen for legal reasons in the battle for incorporation, but to most residents, and to the U.S. Post Office, the area was really La Mirada. The chamber of commerce spearheaded the drive to change Mirada Hills to La Mirada. Andrew McNally had named it well. Petitions were circulated, which qualified the measure for the November 1960 ballot as Proposition T. The chamber of commerce developed a campaign slogan, "Si on 'T'—Viva La Mirada," and 80 percent of the voters were in agreement, giving La Mirada the distinction of being the first city in Los Angeles County to change its name by a vote of its citizens. The name La Mirada became official on December 15, 1960, when the California Secretary of State's Office received and filed the papers mailed from La Mirada.

A survey taken in 1961 by the Jaycees revealed the following characteristics of La Mirada's population: The average household at that time consisted of 4.4 persons; 7 percent of those working held jobs in La Mirada compared

The proposed city of Mirada Hills studied by the zoning board of supervisors in 1960. Supervisor Burton W. Chace sits looking at the map. *Courtesy of Gail Pearce from the La Mirada City Archives.*

to 39 percent who were employed in the city of Los Angeles; 73 percent of the adult men had completed at least one year of college, while 42 percent of the women had accomplished the same; 46 percent of the population held membership in a local church; and 53 percent of the families in the city owned two or more cars. Another survey taken in 1965 revealed that 8.5 percent of the city's working people were employed in La Mirada, 20 percent in Los Angeles and 17 percent in Anaheim and Downey. In 1965, church membership had risen slightly to 50 percent of the community, while 68 percent claimed to attend places of worship.

The deciding factor in 1960. A yes vote would change the name of the city back to La Mirada from Mirada Hills. *Courtesy of Gail Pearce from the La Mirada City Archives.*

La Mirada's population growth was steady but not dramatic during the 1960s. The estimated population in 1963 was 24,900, and in 1965, the city counted approximately 26,700 inhabitants. According to the federal census taken in 1970, La Mirada had 30,808 residents occupying 7,811 residential units. Further details of the 1970 census revealed that 13 percent of the population was of Hispanic origin, women outnumbered men 15,703 to 15,105 and the average household consisted of 3.8 persons. The city's population in 1972 was calculated at 30,974, and the median family income in that year was $13,887. The federal census of 1980 stirred up controversy in the city when the initial figures appeared, showing that La Mirada was considerably smaller than expected. However, these figures were revised upward, and the official count became 40,860 residents occupying 12,494 dwelling units. The average household size continued to decline, standing at 3.2 persons in 1980, and the number of persons of Hispanic origin increased to 19 percent.

While most of the annexations attempted by the city were rather uneventful, a few created a good deal of controversy and not all of them were successful. As early as 1960, some homeowners north of Imperial began an unsuccessful attempt to get out of the new city. The first annexation attempted by Mirada Hills in 1960 failed. A largely uninhabited territory north of Imperial, east

An early 1960s aerial view of the La Mirada Shopping Center and the new La Mirada High School and Golf Course in the surroundings. *Courtesy of Gail Pearce from the La Mirada City Archives.*

of Santa Gertrudes, west of First and south of Leffingwell, did not become part of the city when a majority of the landowners in that area protested the proposed annexation. In January 1961, the Central Manufacturing District, principal opponent of the city's incorporation, praised La Mirada for its efficient management and requested that its remaining property be annexed. In February of the same year, annexation proceedings were initiated for sixteen acres of commercial property at the intersection of Imperial and Santa Gertrudes, and on they went, opening Santa Gertrudes through past Foster Road to Imperial.

A major annexation battle erupted between La Mirada and Whittier in May 1961, in the so-called Greater La Mirada annexation attempt. When

City supervisor Frank G. Bonelli (*center*) and Councilman Richard Danson (*far right*) join county leaders at the ribbon-cutting opening of Santa Gertrudes, 1964. *Courtesy of Gail Pearce from the La Mirada City Archives.*

the proposed city of Whittwood failed to materialize, La Mirada took steps to annex the revenue-creating prize of Whittwood Shopping Center. A newly proposed city of La Colima made it a three-way battle for control of unincorporated East Whittier and the Whittwood Center. The City of Whittier took successful legal action to halt La Mirada's annexation efforts in East Whittier and eventually annexed the area.

On the city's third attempt at annexation, the Windermere area, also known as Mitchell's Island, voted to join the city in the summer of 1969. The following year, annexation proceedings began for the La Pluma area. In March 1971, voters in that district approved of becoming part of La Mirada. The Standard Oil tank farm in northeastern La Mirada was annexed in 1972, paving the way for development of La Mirada's first adult community, La Mirada Landmark.

The city council established a policy later in 1972 that while the city would still be open to annexations by interested property owners, La Mirada would no longer actively seek such annexations. Through homeowners' efforts, the Green Hills area and the Behringer Park area were both brought into the city in 1974.

In June 1975, the city received an annexation request from residents of the Foster Park area. This last annexation to the city also proved to be the most controversial. La Mirada residents and the city council itself were divided over the issue, partly because of an estimated $1 million improvement project that was badly needed on Marquardt Road. Reservations were also expressed concerning the rundown condition of some of the property in the tract, as well as gang activity. This was an argument also used by proponents of annexation who felt the area could be upgraded with city help. In July 1976, the city council voted 3–2 to support Foster Park's annexation if residents of the area could successfully complete the necessary requirements to hold an election. Annexation was still pending in 1977, and the issue was raised that perhaps not only Foster Park should vote on annexation, but also the rest of La Mirada should decide the matter. The timing of the annexation election was also debated. A special election was called in November 1977, and the residents of Foster Park voted by a 5–1 margin to favor annexation. A referendum was then held as part of the March 1978 municipal election to determine how the rest of La Mirada felt about the matter. Voters in La Mirada narrowly approved the Foster Park annexation by a vote of 2,681 to 2,404.

While much of La Mirada was developed at the time of incorporation, there were still several tracts of land within the city awaiting future development. Building permit valuations in the early 1960s demonstrated that development was moving ahead strongly, with $3.6 million worth of construction in 1962 and $4.6 million the following year.

Escalation in the price of homes began slowly and then moved ahead rapidly in the late 1970s. In the subdivision era of the 1950s, a home could often be purchased in La Mirada for as little as $15,000. In 1969, the average La Mirada home was selling for $23,700. By 1973, homes could be found in La Mirada selling for between $25,000 and $75,000, and by the early 1980s, the average La Mirada home was selling for in excess of $100,000. The original Fire Station No. 49 was moved from Valley View Avenue to La Mirada Boulevard next to the Civic Center.

Developments of note included a 310-unit apartment complex known as Los Olivos near the La Mirada Shopping Center. Ground was broken for this, the largest apartment complex ever developed in La Mirada, in December 1971. Seven years later, over the strong protest of many Los

Olivos residents, the complex was given permission from the city to convert to private ownership condominiums. A major development involving 72 townhouses and 98 single-family homes just south of Imperial Highway was also underway in 1971. Another large development of single-family homes was underway in 1978 on the former Standard Oil Company tank farm just east of Santa Gertrudes Avenue in 1978. Several other developments since incorporation have given La Mirada a choice of prices, locations and living styles, although young families just starting out in adult life have found it increasingly difficult to purchase property in La Mirada because of the high cost involved. Those who owned homes in La Mirada were encouraged by high property values, and the pride of ownership was evident in many of the city's residential neighborhoods.

ANNEXATIONS TO THE CITY OF LA MIRADA

Shopping centers at Imperial and Santa Gertrudes—1961
Uninhabited industrial property—1963
Uninhabited industrial property—1964
Uninhabited industrial property—1966
Carwash and restaurant—1967
Windermere area—1969
La Pluma area—1971
Uninhabited area, largely Standard Oil property—1972
Green Hills area—1974
Behringer Park area—1974
Uninhabitated area—1974
One building along Imperial—1974
Foster Park area—1978

PARKS, RECREATION AND CULTURAL ACTIVITIES

La Mirada's desire to become a well-balanced community even before incorporation can be seen in the concern for parks. For three years after subdivision began, there were no parks in La Mirada, but in the remaining years prior to incorporation, three parks were established and a fourth one came into existence the same year cityhood was achieved. La Mirada's parks were under the administrator of the Southeast Park District, later known as the Southeast Recreation and Park District. William Neff leased 4 acres of his 10-acre estate to the community for use as a park for a token fee, giving La Mirada its first park, which opened in 1957. The rest of the land on which the Neff Home stands was later donated to the community by the Neff family. Also in 1957, Windermere Park, once the site of another ranch headquarters, became La Mirada's second park. The third park established was Gardenhill Park, which came about in 1959 when 5 acres were purchased by the park district adjacent to the Gardenhill School site. Frontier Park at Foster Road and Marquardt was opened in June 1960. A large county park in the middle of La Mirada came closer to reality when, in 1959, the county paid $832,000 for 102 acres for what was to become La Mirada Regional Park.

The 1960s saw considerable activity related to park and recreational needs. A community recreation center was constructed at Gardenhill Park in that year, and Los Angeles County awarded a $426,900 contract for construction of the La Mirada Golf Course, with the groundbreaking ceremony held in March. That facility opened in 1963. In the fall of 1961, the city took initial steps that ultimately led to the creation of La Mirada Creek Park. Early 1962 witnessed the groundbreaking for Behringer Park. The value

La Mirada, California, Winterfest 1993. Another yearly event at Behringer Park for the kids. *Courtesy of Gail Pearce from the La Mirada City Archives.*

of maintaining a joint park district with Norwalk and Santa Fe Springs was first called into serious question by La Mirada's city council in 1963. This became an ongoing and at times rather heated issue that was not to be resolved for several years. In March 1964, the Gardenhill Park amphitheater was dedicated, and in June of that year, the groundbreaking was held for the swimming pool complex at La Mirada Regional Park. The pool, which served the community at large, also provided La Mirada High School with a facility for swimming classes and water sports and was dedicated in 1965. Construction began on La Mirada Creek Park in 1964. This park, which included several dams and a concrete channel for the creek, originally contained a lake. However, the lake stagnated and was drained at the request of local residents. In 1965, Creek Park won first place for "most innovative design" in the Los Angeles County beautification campaign.

In the fall of 1965, a contract was awarded for the remodeling of the barn in Neff Park. This was accomplished in such a way as to retain the historical value of the building while at the same time providing the community with a multiuse facility, including a little theater. In March 1969, the county approved final plans for La Mirada Regional Park, and ground was broken in July for development of seventy-three acres with a price tag of $1.3 million. In September 1971, County Supervisor Frank G. Bonelli officiated at the park's dedication.

The La Mirada Stadium was another project initiated in the 1960s. A study was undertaken in 1968 by the Norwalk–La Mirada School District at the request of local residents who saw the need for a stadium in the city. The school district concluded that such a stadium would be best located at La Mirada High School, and it was estimated that the project would cost $400,000–$500,000. The following year, serious discussions were begun between the school district, park district, city officials and local residents over the future stadium. An election was held in August 1971 that created a special stadium assessment district, but at the same time, the bond issue to finance the stadium was voted down. After failure of the bond issue, a joint powers agreement involving the City of La Mirada, the Southeast Recreation and Parks District and the Norwalk–La Mirada Unified School District was worked out whereby the city would advance the money required for construction and be repaid as revenues became available. Eighteen bidders vied for the stadium construction, and a contract was awarded by the city council in October 1972. Although the construction site was vandalized on several occasions, work progressed well, and the 8,200-seat facility was dedicated on October 3, 1973, with a crowd of five thousand in attendance. The dedication program involved drill teams, young athletes, speeches, bands, fireworks and a standing ovation for Ralph Davis, who spearheaded the drive for a stadium and chaired the La Mirada Stadium Commission.

Other parks and recreation developments included the installation of lights on the athletic fields at La Mirada Regional Park in 1970 for a privately owned miniature golf, trampoline and game center on Imperial Highway and establishment and eventual cancellation of the Teen Beat concert program at Gardenhill Park, which proved to be a trouble spot on occasion with larger-than-expected crowds. The Parks and Recreation Commission proposed a horse trail for Creek Park in 1971 as the first step in a proposed larger system of trails in the city, but disappointment came when the county refused to permit a riding trail in the regional park.

July 4, 1973, was the date of the first city-sponsored Independence Day picnic at La Mirada Regional Park. Activities included food booths, games, a regatta of radio-controlled boats on the park's lake and a fireworks display that was less spectacular than planned after automatic sprinklers came on and damaged some of the rockets.

La Mirada Regional Park Pond, 1972. Kids are with their parents operating remote controlled boats. *Courtesy of Gail Pearce from the La Mirada City Archives.*

Also in 1973, the park district began negotiating with heirs of the McNally estate for additional land in the Behringer Park area. Twelve acres were purchased in November of that year for $270,000. Norwalk voted to remain in the Southeast Recreation and Parks District in 1973, but La Mirada was divided over the issue, with some residents feeling that La Mirada was paying more into the district than the city's fair share. However, a consultant's report of that same year did not favor dissolution of the district, and La Mirada continued to support it. Mistreatment of the ducks at the regional park lake became a concern in the 1970s, as maimed ducks were discovered periodically. Parks and recreation commissioner Eric Barker launched a crusade to protect and feed the ducks adequately.

Plans to extend Creek Park along Los Flores Avenue were abandoned in 1974 when residents of the area did not wish to dedicate as much land to the city as had been hoped for. Two new attractions opened at the regional park in 1976: the Frisbee Golf Course, one of the first such facilities in the country, and the bicycle motocross course, added in 1977 with much of the labor provided by Biola College student volunteers.

Following a year of study, the Behringer Park Advisory Committee released a report in May 1976 calling for the development of that facility into an athletic field park. The need for such a facility became evident as areas once in use by youth athletic teams became unavailable. Cor Van Dam, for example, leased a portion of his Valley View Farms land to the La Mirada Little League for many years for $1 per year, but he needed the land for expansion of the dairy in 1977. Finally, in 1982, a $1 million contract was awarded for the redevelopment of Behringer Park, and work was completed the following year.

At Neff Park, tours of the historic Neff house began on Sundays in the summer of 1977. In January 1978, the Neff and George Homes at Neff Park were approved as a National Historic District, largely through the efforts of city historian Bob Camp.

In 1978, an extension of Creek Park south of Imperial Highway resulted when the Oakcreek Homeowners asked for city council support to get the park district to take over their community greenbelt as a public park. A major renovation of Frontier Park was completed in February 1979. In 1980, La Mirada became the first city in California to contract for recreation services, and the recreation services have grown to include very popular events for the children of La Mirada, such as Halloween activities and the annual Easter egg hunt.

Historical Committee members (*left to right*): Don Remley, Lela Criswell, Betty Evans, Chairman Bob Camp, Mary Benton, Mamie Remley and Ned Peebler, 1970. *Courtesy of Gail Pearce from the La Mirada City Archives.*

Youth athletic programs have long been an important part of La Mirada life. Football, soccer, baseball and softball are some of the sports that have involved hundreds of local youths each year as well as many devoted coaches, assistants and parents. For several years, La Mirada hosted the Olive Bowl, a Pop Warner football classic that pitted a leading La Mirada team against a team from a visiting city, often from out of state. The level of interest in youth sports in this community was evidenced in May 1977 when over five hundred people marched on city hall to protest the park district's proposed plan to eliminate baseball and football fields at Behringer Park. Over the years, La Mirada has produced some championship teams in several sports in both school sports and youth sports.

The desire for cultural enrichment has taken many different forms in La Mirada over the years. A branch of the Los Angeles County Public Library was located in the La Mirada Shopping Center and served the community well until 1971. In July 1971 the new, much larger library at the Civic Center

Fiesta de Artes is held at Rosecrans Avenue at the open mall, early 1970s. It was held annually for many years. *Courtesy of Gail Pearce from the La Mirada City Archives.*

opened its doors. In 1961, the city council established a citizens' committee to promote art and culture. This committee, with the support of the Shopping Center Merchants Association, established an annual art festival. The committee also laid the groundwork for the Community Playhouse and the La Mirada Symphony.

The first La Mirada Art Festival was held outdoors at the La Mirada Shopping Center in 1961. The La Mirada Ebell Club was instrumental in this show, as was the city, which proclaimed "Art Week" to publicize the event. The festival boasted 205 entries with prize money of $300. The art show was continued and expanded in 1962 under the name La Mirada Fiesta de Artes. The festival took on an exotic air in 1969 as thirty six-foot Mayan masks were placed along Rosecrans Avenue and the La Mirada Shopping Center to publicize the event. It appeared that the Fiesta de Artes might become a thing of the past in 1970 as the city, deluged with requests from various local organizations, voted to withhold funding. A few weeks later, however, funding was restored and the art show continued. An elaborate Mayan temple scene was created in the shopping center plaza as a focal point for the festival in 1971, the same year that strong winds knocked down a tent and damaged several paintings. By 1972, the festival had grown to include 1,200 entries, an art auction, a dramatic production by La Mirada

Fiesta de Artes, 1972. After demonstrating fascinating techniques, the artists engage the kids in attendance. *Courtesy of Gail Pearce from the La Mirada City Archives.*

High School, a marionette show and Mexican folk dances. An amateur film festival was added in 1973.

After completion of the La Mirada Stadium, the Fiesta de Artes was held at that location briefly and then moved to the La Mirada Civic Theatre and adjacent parking area in 1978. In 1981, the annual event was renamed the La Mirada Festival of Arts. The city has continued to support the art festival, in part by purchasing a painting from the entries submitted each year. Thus the city is developing its own art collection, which is on display in city hall and La Mirada Civic Theatre.

The La Mirada Playhouse was organized in 1960. Sponsored jointly by the city and the Southeast Recreation and Parks District, the Playhouse held dramatic productions at Neff Barn in 1966 prior to the completion of the Civic Theatre.

The La Mirada Symphony became a reality when the premiere concert was given on April 24, 1964. This was preceded by much hard work on the part of a group of interested citizens known as the La Mirada Symphony Association. The orchestra practiced and performed on the Biola College campus until the Civic Theatre became available. Many outstanding guest artists have performed with the symphony over the years. Contributions from the city and many interested citizens continue to make the La Mirada Symphony, under the musical leadership of Leon Guide, a major cultural force in the community.

Steps were taken in 1964 to promote greater international understanding on the part of La Miradans through involvement in the growing Sister City program. In that year, the city of Imatra, Finland, on the border with the Soviet Union, was selected. Contacts between Imatra and La Mirada never developed to the degree hoped for, however, and plans were made in 1973 for the acquisition of another sister city, this time a bit closer to home. At a champagne reception held in March 1973, the Sister City Association announced the country from which a sister city would be selected, El Salvador in Central America. The following month, Santa Tecla was named a sister city, and the mayor of that community came to La Mirada on an official visit. A year later, in April 1974, a group of twenty-six La Miradans reciprocated with a visit to Santa Tecla. In 1980, the Sister City Association sought an additional sister city for La Mirada, this time in Japan. The city of Isehara was selected, and in April 1984, a delegation of seventy-five La Miradans visited that city in a sports and cultural exchange program.

A major cultural development for La Mirada was the construction of the La Mirada Civic Theatre, which the Los Angeles Times called "La Mirada's Jewel" shortly after the facility opened. In September 1975, the La Mirada Redevelopment Agency leased the former movie theater for $40,000 with an option to buy it. Shortly thereafter, the agency agreed on a $1.5 million plan to convert the structure into a 1,300-seat civic theater. In November 1975, architectural drawings were submitted to the city, and the city council began discussing a name for the future auditorium. Actual construction on the theater began in April 1976. By July, it was clear that the cost of revamping the theater was going to exceed the original budget. Construction and decorating costs continued to rise, and when the facility was completed, nearly $3.4 million had been expended. In November 1976, the city hired Thomas Mitze to manage the theater, now officially known as the La Mirada Civic Theatre. A theater board and a support group known as the Friends of the Theatre were appointed by the city council. A sell-out grand opening was held on Friday, September 16, 1977, featuring Tony Bennett and Les Brown and his Band of Renown. The following month, the newly named

Opening in 1977, this is the renowned La Mirada Civic Theatre. Today, the world-famous theater is called the La Mirada Center for the Performing Arts. *Courtesy of Gail Pearce from the La Mirada City Archives.*

Whittier–La Mirada Light Opera Association made the Civic Theatre its home and opened with a production of *Brigadoon*. For the city's nineteenth birthday, a sculpture was commissioned for the grounds of the Civic Theatre and created by noted sculptor Dr. Joseph Young. The towering sculpture known as *Canto '79* cost $35,000, which stirred some controversy at the time, but the artwork has become a noted city landmark. The success of the La Mirada Civic Theatre has been beyond expectations. Of great benefit to the community and the Southland in general, the theater has hosted a wide variety of culturally enriching and entertaining programs in the beautiful facility. In 1980, the Civic Theatre surpassed the 500,000-attendance mark.

Commercial Development

Commercial activity in La Mirada is older than the subdivisions of the 1950s, although in the early years it was very limited in scope. The oldest business in La Mirada is Olive Lawn Memorial Park, which dates to the 1920s. Flower farms, some until recently, also dotted the area in the early years of development. Cor Van Dam's Valley View Farms dairy was in operation

A 1959 aerial of the $5 million La Mirada Shopping Center. *Courtesy of Gail Pearce from the La Mirada City Archives.*

in the early 1950s before subdivision began. A handful of businesses and a couple of supermarkets were in existence prior to incorporation, but most of La Mirada's commercial activity came after incorporation in 1960.

A major addition to the La Mirada Shopping Center occurred when Ohrbachs opened a large $3 million department store in 1960. That year also saw the completion of a facility for Coast Hardboard Inc., La Mirada's first non-farm industry. Groundbreaking for the La Mirada Hospital at Imperial Highway and Telegraph Road was held in September 1960, and the facility opened the following year. The Boys' Market at Imperial and Luitwieler (now La Mirada Boulevard) held its grand opening in November 1960, and the following month, a new Safeway, which became Moskatel's, opened its doors a few hundred yards to the west of Boys'. Apparently La Miradans liked to eat, for many of the businesses established in 1960–61 were food-oriented. The House of Pancakes opened at the La Mirada Shopping Center in February 1961—only the sixth restaurant established in that vast chain now known as the International House of Pancakes, or IHOP.

La Miradans had yet another supermarket when the community's second Market Basket opened at the La Mirada Shopping Center in March 1961, which became a Service Merchandise Showroom. Ground was broken for

Commercial work at the new Ohrbachs Department store, 1959. *Courtesy of Gail Pearce from the La Mirada City Archives.*

an Alpha Beta market at Imperial and Santa Gertrudes in August 1961 and a Von's Market that turned into a Marshall's across the Avenue two months later.

At the La Mirada Shopping Center, ground was broken in January 1962 for the $1 million, 1,200-seat Stanley-Warner Theatre, La Mirada's first movie house (which became the La Mirada Civic Theatre and today the La Mirada Theatre for the Performing Arts). The theater was delayed, because in its construction, there were protests of other theaters from Buena Park to Downey, which feared loss of business due to the new facility.

That same month, the city asked the management of the La Mirada Shopping Center to investigate traffic problems at the center after several accidents involving bicycles and automobiles.

Other commercial developments in the 1960s included the opening of La Mirada Savings and Loan, a locally owned and managed institution, the opening of the Hormel Meat plant in the industrial area of the city in 1964 and the opening of La Mirada's only auto dealership, Patterson Chevrolet, in 1966, which became Werren Chevrolet in 1982. There was also a growing realization that unless a major department store could be attracted, the future of the La Mirada Shopping Center was likely to be too limited. Improvement was seen in this regard when it was announced in 1969 that Woolco would build a $900,000 store at the center. In October 1969, the ninety-nine-bed La Mirada Christian Convalescent Hospital opened. Meanwhile, the industrial area in southern La Mirada had been expanding rapidly so that by 1969 there were 120 industrial firms in the city. American Electric Company was the largest industrial employer in the city at this time with a workforce of 1,200 people.

In 1970, the chamber of commerce moved to new quarters on Imperial Highway. Construction on the Imperial Medical Plaza was started in the fall of 1971 at about the same time the sixty-five-acre Ford Pre-delivery Service facility opened in the industrial section. Also in 1971, the La Mirada Shopping Center underwent a facelift with new landscaping and lighting as well as redesigned traffic patterns. A comparative study of commercial activity for 1971 showed that La Mirada had record taxable sales of $15.4 million in the third quarter of the year, but the city still had the lowest commercial activity of any city in the area. It was clear that many La Miradans shopped elsewhere. An Ohrbachs store opened at the new Cerritos Shopping Center in March 1972, and because of this, the La Mirada Ohrbachs cut its retail space and staff by two-thirds. The year 1973 saw the opening of Carl's Jr. at the La Mirada Shopping Center and the opening of the headquarters of Denny's Restaurants. A chamber of commerce survey showed that as of August 1973, the city's industrial area contained 137 firms employing 6,000 people.

The La Mirada Shopping Center changed ownership in January 1974. New owner Mark Tanz promised that by September of that year, so many improvements would have taken place in the center that it would be hardly recognizable. One change was that Ohrbachs closed its doors completely in the summer of 1974, paving the way for that facility to become the core of a new enclosed mall area. In January 1976, Newberry's closed at the shopping center, and Roberts Department Store moved into that vacancy in August. A September 1976 chamber of commerce survey revealed that the industrial area of La Mirada had now grown to 180 companies employing a workforce of 7,000. That same year, Albertson's opened on La Mirada Boulevard south of Imperial.

In 1977, the first savings and loan institution in La Mirada, Home Savings, expanded into a new facility on Rosecrans Avenue dubbed the "Taj Mahal." The Far East Broadcasting Company broke ground for an office building on Imperial Highway in the spring of 1978. La Mirada's first supermarket, the Market Basket at Rosecrans and Valley View, closed its doors in November 1978, and the building was taken over by the Pep Boys auto store. The Boys' Market on Imperial Highway was demolished in 1978 to make room for the new Gemco center.

Moviegoers were given more choices at the La Mirada Mall theaters when two new larger theaters were added to the complex in 1980. The 1980 chamber of commerce survey of the La Mirada industrial area showed 8,280 persons employed by 218 firms. Two of the city's ailing shopping areas upgraded in 1980: the Imperial Center, site of the closed Food King market, and the center at Imperial and Telegraph. The La Mirada Mall began a transition to a discount mall, the first of its kind in Southern California in 1981. In that same year, work was begun on the revitalization of the Alondra Shopping Center. To the delight of La Mirada's younger set, Toys R Us opened a new store in part of the old Woolco building at the La Mirada Mall in September 1983. The city council and staff were delighted as well, for the new store did a booming business that Christmas and produced considerable sales tax revenue for the city. April 1984 saw the opening of La Mirada's first hotel, the Gateway Holiday Inn at Valley View and the Santa Ana Freeway. A few months later, the Gateway Five Theatres complex opened. In 1984, the La Mirada Mall was purchased by J. Allen Radford in partnership with Long Beach Savings and Loan.

Holiday Inn opened its doors in 1984. *Courtesy of Gail Pearce from the La Mirada City Archives.*

La Mirada was planned without a traditional downtown district and has instead developed a major shopping mall and other neighborhood shopping centers. Some commercial enterprises have flourished while others have struggled and not survived. The city continues to be faced with the challenge of attracting businesses that La Miradans will desire to support. Major upgrading of many of the shopping areas in the city within the last few years has greatly enhanced the appearance of the community. The industrial area, which has evolved into a major warehouse and distribution center, is separated from the residential sections of the city and has been developed according to high standards of aesthetics.

EDUCATION

The story of La Mirada's public schools has been one of rapid growth in the early years of the community's development, followed by a decline

At McNally Intermediate School, teacher Andrew Gray is having a show and tell, 1974. *McNally Intermediate School Yearbook of 1974.*

in enrollment necessitating numerous school closures. Few issues have affected La Miradans as strongly as that of the closing of some of our public schools.

Beginning with the Foster Road School in 1954, five elementary schools were constructed in La Mirada within about a two-year period. High school students were bused to Norwalk, creating the Norwalk–La Mirada Unified School District until La Mirada High School opened its doors in September 1960. One of the first major issues facing the new city government in 1960 was whether or not the city should fund crossing guards for busy streets near elementary schools. Mothers at Gardenhill School took the initiative and organized their own crossing guard patrol until the city council agreed to fund the program for the city.

The growth of La Mirada made it apparent that a new high school would eventually be needed in the community. In January 1961, the high school district filed condemnation proceedings on a forty-acre parcel along Alondra Boulevard near the railroad tracks and Stage Road as the site for a future high school. For safety reasons, the city protested the selection of this site. Before it was over, the high school district had studied ten sites for a second La Mirada high school, including a parcel in Orange County, which was not well received by Buena Park residents. In May 1961, the district moved ahead with condemnation proceedings on the Alondra site. The city recommended an alternate site at Imperial and Valley View, which eventually was desired by the school district for a possible third local high school. The city council was concerned enough over possible safety hazards connected with the Alondra site that an attempt was made to block state funding for the project. Los Angeles County planners turned down the Alondra site in September 1961, thus placing the decision in the hands of the State Allocations Board. Later in September, the site was given state approval. Neff High School opened its doors on this site in the fall of 1964 as school district and city officials watched carefully to see how students would handle the crossing of Stage

Road, Alondra Boulevard and the railroad tracks. While concern for safety was proper, the students proved that they could do very well in less than ideal pedestrian circumstances. Plans for a third high school to be located on dairy land at Imperial and Valley View were dropped in 1965 after a two-year controversy with the landowners over price.

In 1962, La Mirada High School graduated its first class of seniors. In 1964, the La Mirada Ebell Club, in cooperation with the city, began Youth-in-Government Month, an annual event each spring whereby high school seniors are exposed to the workings of local government and actually assume positions of leadership alongside their official city counterparts at commission and council meetings.

Funding for local public schools became a major story in 1970 when the state cut $560,000 from the allocation expected by the Norwalk–La Mirada School District. This action resulted in the trimming of one period from the academic day at the high schools, cutbacks in school library services and the elimination of school nurses. Another major event of the early 1970s was the decline in elementary age children in the district. As a result, discussions were first held in 1972 to consider the possible closing of some elementary schools. The first La Mirada school targeted for possible closure was Kling School. The district's financial and enrollment woes were evidenced in the dismissal of 114 probationary teachers throughout the district at the end of the 1972 school year. In the fall of 1972, the school district opened an adult education center to Anthony School, over the objections of some of that school's parents.

In 1974, as enrollment in the district continued to drop, the school board took up the unpleasant task of deciding which schools to close in that year. After public hearings in January, in February the board decided that five more schools should close. Three of these were in La Mirada: Kling, Anthony and Los Coyotes Intermediate. It was not an easy year for the board in the Norwalk–La Mirada Unified School District. Upset over school closures and the reassignment of personnel, parents launched an active, though unsuccessful recall movement aimed at all seven of the board members. When it was determined by the board that the Los Coyotes campus should be used for the El Camino Continuation School, some local residents protested. When school opened in the fall of 1974, the district's enrollment was less than twenty-five thousand students, the lowest in fifteen years. La Mirada High School held a sit-in shortly after school opened to protest a new, more stringent dress code.

The district's enrollment and financial difficulties continued. Additional teacher layoffs were required in 1975. Some who hoped for improved school funding felt seen when the California Supreme Court ruled in 1977 that the method of financing public schools based on local property taxes was unconstitutional. The decision worked to the advantage of the Norwalk–La Mirada District, which suffered from an inadequate tax base. In May 1977, Norwalk–La Mirada teachers and the board reached an impasse in contract talks and a state mediator was requested.

Faced with a continued enrollment decline, the school district formed a citizens' group to make recommendations for additional school closures. In February 1978, over 1,500 people jammed the school closure meeting at which a new grade system was announced. Elementary schools would in the future cover grades kindergarten to seventh, the intermediate schools would be eliminated and high schools would include the eighth graders. The plan necessitated a massive transfer of personnel between schools. The school district, alarmed at what the proposed Proposition 13 on the June ballot might do to school financing, urged voters to defeat the measure. When Proposition 13 passed, the school board froze salaries for the following year and canceled summer school for 1978. When school opened in the fall of 1978, only twenty-six schools were open in a district that had once contained thirty-seven.

The issue of school segregation became a major concern in 1978–79. According to state guidelines, half of the district's schools were racially segregated, and the district was under pressure to work out a desegregation plan by the fall of 1979. In January 1979, the Norwalk–La Mirada School District Desegregation Study Committee was formed. Many district parents made it clear from the outset that involuntary busing of students would be unacceptable. The desegregation committee submitted its report in May 1979. The report concluded that there were no segregated schools in the district at that time but that six schools were in danger of becoming segregated. The report was accepted by the school board.

In the face of continuing enrollment declines, the Norwalk–La Mirada Unified School District began a new study of possible school closures in November 1980. In a report that sent shockwaves through the community, an administrative committee suggested in January 1981 that La Mirada High School and Excelsior High School be closed at the end of the school. After public hearings and much deliberation, the school district decided to keep La Mirada High School open and close Neff High School and Excelsior High School. Mesa and Rancho Schools were also slated for closure at the final meeting on school closures, attended by over one thousand people. Neff students wept and sang their alma mater at the close of the meeting, amid hopes that the transition to a single La Mirada high school would

The Neff High School drill team out in front of Neff High School. *Neff High School Yearbook of 1969.*

be a smooth one. Neff High School was demolished in 1983 as part of a redevelopment project for the industrial area. Two impressive affairs happened at Neff High School. Bridget Gregory and Elizabeth Vargas Stitt led the Neff High School drill team. The team and the Neff High School band were a sight to see as they marched and played at every city parade. The city leaders asked for their participation annually. The other inspiring undertaking was a Neff student named Kenneth Smith. With his talent for making hard clay projects, in 1974 and finishing in 1975, Kenneth started and worked never stopping until he constructed a robust statue. It was called *Tommy Trojan*, and the Neff High School teams were called the Trojans.

The making of *Tommy Trojan*, the statue, at Neff High School by Kenneth J. Smith, 1975–76. *Kenneth J. Smith collection.*

What Kenneth made was the mascot statue of the school, and there it stood prominently outdoors.

Despite the difficulties facing the public schools, several private schools, including a growing number of preschools, have prospered in La Mirada. Most of these schools have had a church affiliation and have provided a viable alternative to public education.

La Mirada also contains one institution of higher education, Biola University. Biola was founded in 1908 by Lyman Stewart, co-founder and president of the Union Oil Company. Known originally as the Bible Institute of Los Angeles (hence the acronym BIOLA), the school was located in downtown Los Angeles and was designed primarily as a training ground for pastors, missionaries and other Christian workers. The school gradually expanded its curriculum and became a four-year Bible college, then added several liberal arts programs as well. Under the leadership of President Samuel H. Sutherland, the school decided to move from its overcrowded

Biola College invited the students from McNally School next door to etch their names in the wet cement, 1963. *Courtesy of Gail Pearce from the La Mirada City Archives.*

Biola University, also known as the Bible Institute of Los Angeles, circa 2000s. *Courtesy of Gail Pearce from the La Mirada City Archives.*

downtown location to the suburbs. After several possible sites for a new campus were investigated, La Mirada was selected. Over one hundred acres in the middle of La Mirada were purchased in the mid-1950s for $4,500 per acre. The school later sold off part of its holdings to finance campus construction. The school, known as Biola College, and its graduate school, Talbot Theological Seminary, held a groundbreaking ceremony for the new campus in 1957. The new campus opened in the fall of 1959 with 753 students in attendance. Within a decade, the college's enrollment was 1,425, and a peak enrollment of 3,200 was reached in 1980. Dr. Sutherland retired as president of the college in 1970 after thirty-five years with the institution. He was replaced in that office by Dr. J. Richard Chase, who served until 1982. During Dr. Chase's presidency, the school changed its name to Biola University, a name more accurately reflecting the programs of the institution, which by then included several master's degree programs as well as doctorates in clinical psychology and theological studies. Biola has retained many of the Christian elements distinctive of the Biola College days while expanding the curriculum over the years. Many La Miradans have enjoyed concerts, dramatic presentations, lectures and other special events sponsored by Biola over the years. Dr. Clyde Cook has served as president of the university since 1982.

MORE EVENTS AND ISSUES

La Mirada established one major community tradition even before the city's incorporation. Known as the La Mirada Gras, this annual event was established in 1956 by the chamber of commerce and the Jaycees. A combination town fair, carnival and talent and beauty contest, the La Mirada Gras also included a parade along Rosecrans Avenue to the La Mirada Shopping Center by 1960. The parade was televised on channel 11 in 1961 and featured Jayne Mansfield as grand marshal. Mr. and Miss La Mirada were selected each August to preside over the festivities. In 1965, the chamber of commerce suggested that the La Mirada Gras and the art festival merge, inasmuch as the art festival was doing more for the city's image than the carnival.

Expo La Mirada was another community tradition, begun in 1967 by the chamber of commerce. Booths and exhibits featuring the services and products of La Mirada businesses and industry were set up in the gymnasium at Biola College for the public to see. Other community events beginning in the 1960s included the annual home Christmas lighting contest sponsored by the Jaycees, which lasted until the energy crisis of 1973; the Angel Tree project, which collected Christmas gifts for needy La Mirada area youngsters; the haunted house sponsored each Halloween by the Children's Home Society, which drew thousands of visitors annually; and the Fiesta de Mayo, a parade and carnival similar to the La Mirada Gras that was revived briefly in 1969 by the Jaycees.

Other events of significance in the 1960s include the construction of Temple Beth Ohr as a place of worship for La Mirada's Jewish community in 1961; the establishment of an organization called Mothers of Mirada Servicemen (MOMS), which sent birthday cards, Christmas gifts and other tokens of support from the community to La Miradans serving in the armed forces; and the renaming of Luitwieler Avenue to La Mirada Boulevard in 1966. November 1969 marked the end of an era for home-delivered baked goods when Helms Bakery went out of business.

Fires have played a part in the history of La Mirada, although fortunately the loss of life has been minimal. In addition to residential fires, several major commercial and industrial fires have been experienced by the community. In March 1969, two teenagers with firecrackers were responsible for a $250,000 oil fire at the Standard Oil tank farm near Dulles School as fourteen thousand barrels of crude oil went up in smoke. A fire determined to be the result of arson destroyed several shops in April 1970 at the Mirada

West Shopping Center at Valley View and Imperial, causing $250,000 in damage. A $20,000 fire occurred at the La Mirada Country Club in January 1971. Six shops in the Green Hills Shopping Center were gutted by fire in July 1973, including Spence's Bike Shop and Gondola Pizza. On Halloween night in 1974, a freight train derailed while passing through La Mirada, causing a propane car to explode in flames. A one-square-mile residential area of the city was evacuated as a precaution. In November 1975, a fire and explosion did $300,000 worth of damage to the AMSCO Chemical Corporation on Alondra Boulevard, causing evacuation of part of the city's industrial district as well as a nearby residential area. Valley View Farms suffered a major hay fire in January 1976, one of several experienced by La Mirada's only dairy. A toxic waste storage yard at Marquardt and Imperial in Santa Fe Springs, just a stone's throw from the La Mirada border, burned in July 1981, hurling flaming fifty-five-gallon drums into the air. Toxic waste ran into the nearby flood control channel and traveled all the way to Seal Beach, forcing closure of the public beach there. Cleanup operations funded by the Environmental Protection Agency took six months. For months afterward, local residents complained of health problems brought on by the fire. Another major blaze destroyed the Alondra Market in October 1981.

La Mirada's tenth birthday celebration in March 1970 was a major event. Festivities included a 140-entry parade televised on KTLA, a giant birthday cake, a fireworks display and a Birthday Ball at the Los Coyotes Country Club. In May 1970, the new La Mirada Post Office opened at the La Mirada Mall. La Mirada traditions of the 1970s included the annual Thanksgiving Service sponsored by the La Mirada Clergy Association, the annual Memorial Day service sponsored by the VFW at Olive Lawn Memorial Park and the annual dog vaccination clinic held each summer at La Mirada High School. La Miradans themselves lined up for vaccinations against the dreaded swine flu epidemic, which failed to materialize in the mid-1970s. Local pride swelled in March 1972 when sixteen-year-old Neff High School student Debbie Heald set the women's world record for running an indoor mile at the U.S. and Russian indoor track meet in Richmond, Virginia.

In late 1973, the effects of an energy crisis began to be felt. A carpool information board was set up in city hall in January 1974 as gasoline became increasingly expensive and more difficult to get. Many La Miradans awoke before dawn to wait in line at local gas stations, which usually sold out of their daily allotments within a short time. The July 4 picnic and fireworks show at La Mirada Regional Park was an established tradition by the mid-1970s. Skydivers landing in the park also became part of the Independence Day festivities. Eleven persons were arrested at the July 4, 1975, celebration after a disturbance involving the throwing of rocks and bottles at sheriff's deputies.

La Mirada's fifteenth birthday celebration in 1975 included a town meeting at city hall where residents were divided into groups and asked to openly discuss their likes and dislikes concerning life in La Mirada. Frequently mentioned "likes" included the city's cleanliness and upkeep, the small-town atmosphere, the Dial-A-Ride system, parks and a responsive city government. Dislikes included inadequate shopping facilities, smog, lack of adequate regional rapid transits and lack of dinner restaurants, inadequate police protection and a degree of dissatisfaction with the public schools.

8

DIAL-A-RIDE SERVICE MAY SOLVE BUS PROBLEM

San Bernardino Sun, October 1, 1973

By Robert Lindsey, "New York Times News Service"

La Mirada, CA–Interview with Freda Terenzio, a La Mirada Citizen

La Mirada—Mrs. Freda Terenzio sat down in her kitchen, dialed 943-6776 and told the man at City Hall that she wanted to go to Von's Market.

Larry Samdow, the dispatcher at City Hall scanned a huge map that looked as if it might have come from a military war room. Instead of troops, the markers on the map denoted buses. He spotted a bus cruising near her home and replied, "We'll be there in 10 minutes."

Mrs. Terenzio was a customer of La Mirada's new "Dial-A-Ride" system, a successful example of a transit innovation that is spreading across the Country.

As the bus pulled away from her home later, Mrs. Teenzio dropped a quarter in the fare box, turned to another passenger and said:

"This is really something. It's cheaper than a taxi, but it's better than the bus."

In inaugurating dial-a-ride services, Officials are trying to entice motorists out of their cars and to provide public transportation for people who do not have cars.

Dial-a-Ride, a big success, 1973. La Mirada was the first city in the U.S. to operate a safe transit service for its residents. *Courtesy of Gail Pearce from the La Mirada City Archives.*

"When people realize how it works, it will spread like wildfire—provided people make the commitment to pay for it," said William Drake, a University of Michigan professor of Urban Planning.

The 12 and 18–passenger buses that roll through La Mirada, a six-square-mile city of 32,000 just south of Los Angeles, have no fixed routes. Instead, they go where the demand is greatest at different times of day.

A two-man dispatcher team takes pick-up requests, locates the bus nearest the caller and instructs the driver over a two-way radio where to go next. Pick-ups and drop-offs in the same parts of town are grouped to reduce wasted driving.

La Mirada Officials here and elsewhere say they believe it fills a need, especially for people without access to a car—the elderly, the young, the poor and the handicapped.

9

LA MIRADA INTRODUCES ENORMOUS BANNERS OF ALL THIRTY-EIGHT PRESIDENTS AND THE SETTING OF THE TIME CAPSULE

In the bicentennial year of 1976, all of the presidents were displayed on a magnificent banner strung from light poles on La Mirada Boulevard. A time capsule was placed in the wall of the Civic Theatre, to be opened in the year 2176. Other events of local interest in the 1970s included two La Mirada High School students setting a world record for skateboarding in June 1976. Kevin Walker and Terry Bates traveled 73.6 miles from Long Beach City Hall to the San Diego city limits in twelve hours. The La Mirada Mall, the city and the chamber of commerce sponsored La Mirada's first Christmas parade in December 1976. Heavy rains in March 1978 brought flash flooding and mudslides to La Mirada near the end of a rainy season that dumped over thirty inches of precipitation on the city. Property taxes were on the minds of many in La Mirada after most of the city was reassessed by the county tax assessor in 1978. The unpleasant prospect of taxes doubling or tripling helped popularize the cause of Proposition 13, the property tax rollback initiative. The La Mirada Civic Theatre hosted a debate on Proposition 13 between Howard Jarvis and State Senator Peter Behr, moderated by President J. Richard Chase of Biola College. The La Mirada Civic Theater evolved into one of the top Broadway–style houses for award-winning plays now called the La Mirada Theater for the Performing Arts. The 1970s also saw annual spring home tours of some of La Mirada's loveliest residences, sponsored as a scholarship fundraiser by the La Mirada

La Mirada Boulevard, 1976. *Courtesy of Gail Pearce from the La Mirada City Archives.*

The Company Dancers and *Singers of Seven Brides for Seven Brothers*, a vibrant play at the La Mirada Theater for the Performing Arts, circa 2000s. *Courtesy of Gail Pearce from the La Mirada City Archives.*

Ebell Club. The gasoline lines returned to La Mirada in April and May 1979, with the state again adopting an "odd-even" plan whereby the last digit of one's license plate determined which days gasoline could be purchased.

La Miradans were surprised in March 1980 to learn that Dick Hurley, editor of the *La Mirada Lamplighter*, was leaving that post after working for the newspaper for twenty-five years. For years, Hurley editorials kept local residents on their toes and whether or not one agreed with him, it was evident that here was a man who cared about what happened in La Mirada.

10

THE FOLKS AT VALLEY VIEW FARMS PRESENT

1954

Yesteryear La Mirada was characterized by row on row of graceful olive trees. Now for the most part, these trees have been replaced by row on row of beautiful new homes. A once proud ranch becomes a very proud city.

The purchase was for the specific purpose of subdividing 1,500 acres of the land into a country gentlemen farming colony. Even though it fell short of McNally's goal of a farm colony, it has far exceeded his dreams by becoming one of the largest subdivisions for homes in California to date.

It wasn't many months after this that construction began on the first homes of what was destined to become one of Southern California's finest cities in the ten- to fifteen-thousand population classes. Already better than four thousand homes have been built and most of them occupied. Plans are also rapidly being pushed to give La Mirada its own complete shopping center, newspaper, parks and recreation facilities, schools, churches and Bible college.

Another businessman with a vision for the future of this community was Mr. C.A. Van Dam. In May 1952, Mr. and Mrs. Van Dam purchased twenty-six acres at the corner of Valley View Avenue and Rosecrans. This building site was chosen as an ideal location for a modern dairy due to soil topography, central location in the LA milkshed and a sparsely populated farming community. In the construction of Valley View Farms, the most modern milking equipment was installed in order to ensure the highest-quality milk products possible.

The Valley View Farms Dairy Cash and Carry's first uniformed crew, known as Crew AA1. Cor Van Dam, the owner, is at bottom left, 1961. *Cornel Van Dam family collection.*

After operating as a wholesale dairy until January 1954, the folks of Valley View Farms felt a need as a service to the community to establish a cash and carry outlet whereby the increased population of La Mirada could have the benefit of a quality milk product at prices far below market and home delivery costs.

This enterprise became a reality with the opening of Valley View Farms' first unit on January 16, 1954. With the opening of this unit, the residents of La Mirada soon realized the increased value of their milk dollar, necessitating the construction of a second unit to ensure faster, more courteous service and, by the addition of two extra lanes, to eliminate the traffic congestion.

We of Valley View Farms would like to take this opportunity to express our gratitude to our many wonderful customers for their patience and consideration during our expansion program. It is our sincere aim to continue to serve you with the same courteous service and quality products in the future that you have received in the past. And it is in appreciation for your goodness toward us that we prepared this brief history of La Mirada for you.

For gathering the necessary material for this history, we are indebted to Mr. William Neff, manager of McNally Ranch, and our own Jess Smithson, and take this opportunity to publicly thank them both.

11

THE PEEBLERS—BYRON AND ETHEL PEEBLER OF OLIVE LAWN MEMORIAL PARK CEMETERY

Byron Peebler was born December 25, 1887, to John Frederick and Mary Ellen Peebler, pioneer Oregon stock. The first Peebler family emigrated from Peebleshire, Scotland, in the early 1800s to settle first in Iowa before moving in 1851 to homestead in eastern Oregon. Byron's grandfather had been a guard on wagon trains traveling the Oregon Trail. As a youth, Byron lived near Albany, Linn County, Oregon.

On Christmas Day 1907, Byron married Ethel Delancey (born May 18, 1889), and they continued to live in Oregon for the next eleven years. Their first five children, all daughters, were born in Oregon. Misfortune entered their lives when fire destroyed the farmhouse. In 1918, the family moved to Canada, where, Byron had been told, top wages were being paid for tractor drivers in the grain fields. Sorrow again came to the Peebler family when their third born, Alma, passed away in 1921 at their home in Calgary, Alberta. Two sons were born there, Gerald in 1918 and Ned in 1920.

The Peebler family returned to Oregon in 1922, but finances continued to plague the family. The home on the Oregon farm had been rebuilt, and since Byron was unable to raise his share of the rebuilding costs, he turned over his share of the farm to his brother and moved to California in the same year.

Byron found work in California as a carpenter and settled his family in Glendale. They lived in a tent in Glendale, and while he was at work constructing a modest home, fire struck again. Much of their photos and family records were destroyed during this blaze.

Those post–World War I years were not prosperous, as carpenter work was slow and times were difficult, especially for a family of seven children; their last child, daughter Betty, was born in 1924. As Byron stated, "There was no Social Security, no unemployment insurance, none of that. We had to make enough money to eat and if we didn't make enough money we didn't eat. And we had to have clothes to keep warm."

A carpenter friend told Byron of a brother who was a salesman for a cemetery in San Fernando Valley making good wages. This contact led Byron to J.M. Dansinger, owner of a new cemetery in La Mirada. Dansinger had purchased 4 acres and an additional acre later, at the northeast corner of Luitwieler and the dirt lane which later became Alicante Road. He also had an option to buy 160 acres of the land that now the County Regional Park. Included in the option were water rights from the well, now out of service, that furnished necessary water for the plantings on the new cemetery grounds. Pipes had been laid through the land owned by the Jacob Stern family in the attempt to develop much of the area for farming. The well was located east of the Golf Course Club House. Dansinger, to get official sanction and dedication of the project as a cemetery, had six bodies from the County Potters Field brought in and buried during the night. This qualified his land as a cemetery. Such actions were not unusual in those early years.

In 1924, Byron started out as a salesman at the La Mirada office, working the first two months with a supervisor on the days he was not employed in carpenter work. For transportation, he traded a goat for an old Model T Ford touring car without a top. Rain or shine he drove the open automobile on the three-hour round trip from Glendale to La Mirada and back. Soon he devoted all his time to the job, and in four months he was promoted to a sales crew chief with six salesmen under his supervision. When the Model T gave out, he purchased a Chevrolet 490 for seventy dollars. "I really had a good automobile then," Byron boasted. In a few months, he was earning approximately one hundred dollars per week, very good wages in those days. Dansinger had a sales crew of twenty-five salesmen covering Long Beach, Los Angeles and many other communities of Los Angeles County and as far as Lancaster. During the mid-1920s, upward of three hundred burials were made in the new cemetery. This was the new era of cemeteries, when the ground-level grave marker became popular. The La Mirada cemetery, named Graceland Cemetery, never had the upright gravestones of the older cemeteries. A chapel had been planned on a portion of the land, and with the option on the additional 160 acres the project appeared to be successful.

Then starting in 1926, financial problems beset Dansinger. Without ready funds, he was unable to take up the option on the 160 acres, and with the loss of the option, water rights from the well were also lost. Dansinger also lost more funds in the stock market crash of 1929, and he had money invested in the building of the Los Angeles Coliseum for the 1932 Olympic Games.

Further problems had developed in maintaining the cemetery; as there had been no endowment fund set up for the perpetual care, state laws were lax in the controlling of cemeteries. The cemetery was left to revert to nature, and the sales crew sought other jobs. In these years following the close of the cemetery, families of deceased buried in the cemetery had the graves opened and the bodies removed for interment elsewhere. Dansinger did save the original five acres; these had been paid for and deeded to him. However, in the final settlement, he deeded the area to his superintendent, B.C. Olds, for back wages.

During these years the Peebler family moved to Indio, California, where a laundry was established and operated by the family.

Byron's reentry into the cemetery business came in 1931 when Olds contacted him with a proposition to form a partnership and reopen the La Mirada cemetery. Olds did not have funds to organize a company by himself. A three-way partnership—Olds, Byron and Ethel Peebler—was established. In 1932, Byron and Ethel returned to the area, living in a rented house in Buena Park to work on the cemetery. A span of mules and a two-wheeled mower were borrowed to cut the tall grass and weeds. The trees Olds had planted when the cemetery was first opened had never been trimmed and the lower limbs had become a tangled mass on the ground. These were trimmed away, and the piles of grass, weeds and tree limbs were burned. A well was drilled to supply needed water. The cemetery name was also changed from Graceland to Olive Lawn Memorial Park. With the clearing completed and the grounds again neat and clean, Byron and Ethel returned to Indio; Olds remained to manage the cemetery.

So far, the Peebler money and efforts were simply investment with little return, as few burials were made in the following years. In 1935, Olds visited Byron and Ethel at the laundry to inform them that they would have to collect a sum of money by the following Monday, to buy four acres surrounding the cemetery, or someone else would purchase the land and they wouldn't be able to expand. At the time, immediate funds were not available, and on such short notice they wouldn't have time to raise it. What Olds didn't mention, Byron discovered later, was that the other buyer was Dansinger and his wife. She had inherited some money, and the deal was an apparent plan to squeeze out the Peeblers. Dansinger also filed a lawsuit claiming the deed had not been legal. Byron came to La Mirada and discovered that Olds had previously mortgaged a portion of the land originally set aside for the chapel. Unfortunately for the Peeblers, they had accepted Olds's word that the cemetery was free and clear of debts. Byron admits this was a serious mistake on their part. He was able to locate the holder of the mortgage, a Mr. Utterback, and was able to buy back the title on the mortgage, thus clearing that problem. When the contract agreement with Olds was decided in court, Byron was informed that the purchasing of the mortgage would not have been necessary. The litigations with Dansinger, on several issues, extended eleven years. Dansinger lost each suit, and eventually the Peeblers won final judgment and were awarded a sum of $10,680 by the court. Byron and Ethel estimated the entire litigation cost to them was between $15,000 and $20,000.

Following the successful court battles, the Peeblers purchased the four acres in the original squeeze plan and established an endowment fund of $20 per grave site, later raised to $40 for the uninterrupted care of the cemetery. With this established, a working fund of $80,000 was set up to ensure development and future care of the cemetery.

During the years of the legal problems, the cemetery received a bad reputation; few burials were made during this time. It was a case of rebuilding a reputation.

In 1947, Byron and Ethel moved a trailer onto the cemetery for their residence until a home could be built. Framing was completed by the end of that year, but the house was covered only by black tarpaper when the Peeblers held their 1948 Christmas in the kitchen.

Ethel recalls they still had few burials, two or three a month, with some months having none. Even when the subdivision of the McNally Ranch well underway, she remembered hearing rumors that the cemetery was to be condemned.

Byron and Ethel, in reminiscing on the years back to 1924, recalled the only industrial building between Los Angeles and La Mirada was the large tire plant on the then Telegraph Road and Anaheim-Telegraph Road with the striking frontage. It was country with few farmhouses in between. Luitwieler Avenue extended only to the cemetery from Stage Road along the route of present-day Escalona. In the 1920s, the road to La Habra was a dirt path through present-day Regional Park past present-day La Mirada High School to Goodman Avenue and on to La Habra. For many years, the only close neighbors were the Mexican American and Japanese flower growers

Byron and Ethel Peebler, pictured here in 1970, maintained Olive Lawn Memorial Park Cemetery. *Courtesy of Gail Pearce from the La Mirada City Archives.*

living on their farms, which is now Regional Park. Two lived nearby: one to the east on the knoll just beyond today's parking lot for the park, the other to the north on approximately the site of the county library building. Grain fields of the McNally Ranch were on the south, while across Luitwieler (directly across the avenue) were extensive dark olive groves of the McNally Ranch. Imperial Highway was completed across the northern part of the McNally Ranch in the 1930s; Luitwieler was extended from the cemetery to Imperial for linkage with the other portion of Luitwieler extending north to Whittier. The Volkner home was in the southeast corner of Imperial and Luitwieler, while farther to the east was the old Reeve ranch and the McComber Ranch.

Through the years, up to 1969, when grading work was started on the land for the Regional Park, the cemetery was visited by jackrabbits, quail, skunks, opossum and pheasants. Occasionally a coyote would roam through. Snakes were common. Byron recalled the day when a four-foot-long bull snake was found near the house. It was still rural living for the Peeblers; shopping was mostly in Buena Park, although at times they did drive to Norwalk to shop in the stores along Front Street next to the railroad. They also shopped at times in the food market on Telegraph Road across from the Sears Store.

Byron remembered the Santa Fe trains going through La Mirada, the locomotives, the huge engines with the engineer cab on the front of the boilers. The earth would tremble at the cemetery when the trains roared along the track through La Mirada.

During heavy rainstorms, La Mirada Creek would overflow onto the lowlands of the present-day Biola athletic field. Luitwieler Avenue would be closed to traffic. Torrents would also flow through the swales of the land, now the Regional Park and Golf Course. The gulley, which is now filled in for the city hall parking lot, usually ran with a four-foot torrent of water following the rains, and the southwest corner of the cemetery became a quagmire as Luitwieler and the dirt lane, now Alicante, were level with the cemetery. This often forced the Japanese farmers coming from their farms to drive through the cemetery to reach Luitwieler Avenue.

The start of the subdivision of the McNally Ranch in the early 1950s left little impression on the Peeblers. That first development on Alondra by Harold L. Shaw was a mile away and sheltered from the cemetery by the groves. It was only when crews started ripping out the trees along Luitwieler Avenue and grading the road along the cemetery that the Peeblers were really aware of the changes coming to their quiet land.

In 1952, Ned and Edith Peebler joined their father and mother in the operation of the cemetery, taking up residence in a house moved into the northeast corner. Here they resided for twenty-two years, raising their son and daughter. The cemetery was doing very well in the 1950s; an additional 1.4 acres was later purchased from the county land to make the present 10-acre site. In 1968, a garden-type crypt mausoleum was constructed on the south border, and plans were for another mausoleum to eventually be constructed along the rest of the Alicante side and along Luitwieler (at this time La Mirada Boulevard); however, this was discouraged by the city government and future construction never developed. In other matters, Ned and his father became active in community affairs and the La Mirada Chamber of Commerce. Byron and Ethel's other son, Gerald, and his wife, Harriet, and family were running the very first drive-thru Laundromat and Cleaners in Santa Ana, California.

The cemetery was considered successful by the start of the 1970s; perhaps Byron and Ethel had thoughts of retiring after sixty-three years of active life. Retirement, as it developed, was not in their immediate plans. In late 1972, Byron, now approaching his eighty-fifth year and Ethel now eighty-three moved to a farm in Arkansas. The harsh burden of farming would not be entirely on their shoulders; plans were for a young couple to move onto the farm and handle much of the heavy work. Apparently, plans didn't work out too well, and with land prices increasing in a few months, the Peeblers wisely sold the property and moved to a two-acre property on the outskirts of Mountain View, Arkansas.

Sadly, in December 1973, the union was broken with the death of Ethel. She had a brief illness and was in the hospital. Byron had a cot moved into her room, and there they spent their sixty-sixth wedding anniversary and Christmas, by her bedside. Ethel passed away on December 30, 1973.

Funeral services were held for Ethel Peebler at the Norwalk Mortuary Chapel on January 4, 1973, by the Reverend Robert Jones of the Four Square Community Church. She was laid to rest in the garden mausoleum in the family cemetery of Olive Lawn Memorial Park.

In 1974, Ned and Edith Peebler left La Mirada to live in Morongo Valley, California. Also in 1974, Gerald and Harriet Peebler, who had continued the family laundry in Indio until 1946, when they moved to Santa Ana to start up their successful drive-thru Laundry and Cleaners, left Santa Ana and moved to La Mirada to assume management of the cemetery and reside in the house at the entrance of the cemetery.

On July 10, 1977, Byron, still living in Mountain View, married sixty-nine-year-old Tempe Younger, also of Mountain View, Arkansas, in a ceremony attended by most of the Peebler family. They continued residence in Mountain View except for driving trips around the country.

Also in 1977, Gerald and Harriet purchased other family interests in the Olive Lawn Memorial Park and became sole owners and operators. Gerald and Harriet became involved with many community projects. In 1979, Gerald was elected president of the La Mirada Chamber of Commerce. Their son, Scott, assisted in the operation of the cemetery and, with his wife, Vicki, moved into the home formerly occupied by Ned and Edith. That year also saw the construction of a chapel-like roof over the old home at the entrance to provide additional space and straighten out the lines of the building. The perpetual care endowment fund was also increased to sixty dollars per grave site to maintain maintenance in the continuing spiraling inflation rate.

Addendum

Byron Peebler continued his active life with the start of 1980. On an errand to town in the early months of 1980 to obtain parts for his new Model T

Ford he acquired to restore, he was struck by a truck making a left turn at an intersections breaking his ankle and severely bruising the side of his chest, which gave Byron plenty of misery.

On the morning of September 8, he arose early as usual, had breakfast and then mentioned he was nauseated and went to the bathroom. Returning, he settled into a chair. Tempe was alarmed and called the family doctor. Byron apparently was surprised when the doctor arrived. After checking Byron, the doctor left for other calls. Within an hour or so Byron's condition had worsened, and he passed away when the doctor returned. Death was determined as heart failure.

Memorial services were held September 13, 1980, at the Olive Lawn Memorial Park, conducted by Reverend Samuel Sutherland of Biola, where Byron was laid to rest in the mausoleum next to Ethel.

12

THE OLIVE AND ITS OIL THAT STARTED LA MIRADA ENDED IN AN EARTHQUAKE IN 1933

Olives are part of La Mirada's life. When the town was subdivided in the early 1950s, every house in town had an olive tree in its front lawn.

Times have changed since then, but here's the story of olives in La Mirada.

Epicurean delight has been romanticized since the beginning of recorded time. Epicurean means "connoisseur." Andrew McNally said this many times and once published it.

First introduced into California by the Mission padres, olives were proclaimed in the 1880s as an ideal orchard crop, and olives were planted on the farms and ranches of California.

By the 1920s, the olive oil business in La Mirada was declining, although in 1921, sales here in town were $13,239 compared to a 1931 income of $1,204.

So, one says, "Olive pickles, olive oil." What's that?

It's this town's history.

In the early years of the ranch, olive crops were purchased from other growers to supplement McNally's Ranch crop, areas such as Santa Ana, Orange, San Juan Capistrano, Madame Modjeska ranch and the Irvine ranch.

Oil was being shipped throughout the West and into the Midwest to Chicago. In 1905, the sales from La Mirada were $25,672, with $11,000 sold through the Chicago office and paid directly to the McNally estate in La Mirada.

Founder of La Mirada, California, Andrew McNally. *Courtesy of the La Mirada City Archives.*

The year 1933 dealt the final blow to the McNally oil business—the historic Long Beach earthquake.

Although little damage was done to other buildings on the ranch, the olive oil mill was badly shaken and pressing of oil was discontinued.

Soon thereafter, Leonardo Dichiara opened a small fruit stand near the station, purchased the pressing equipment and continued operations on a small scale in a building in the courtyard of the olive plant in La Mirada. Later, Dichiara purchased one of the bunkhouses on the Standard Oil property on Alondra Boulevard and continued oil pressing until the building was destroyed by fire in the 1940s.

This was the end of olive oil pressing in La Mirada.

13

FIRST CITY CLERK

1960–2002

By Alice Palicz

There were many hardworking people who added to happy memories, and in La Mirada, California, there was none more delightful or harder working than Anna J. Martin. My name is Alice Palicz, and I am contentedly presenting to you the history of my good friend Anna J. Martin during La Mirada's incorporation.

Prior to La Mirada's cityhood, Ann was working with Coleman Isaac at City National Bank.

On her own time, she had been helping get things moving for the new city. Coley hated to lose her, but he knew she would be an asset to the new city, so he reluctantly let her leave his employment.

After the first city council was sworn in, their first action was to pass a resolution establishing Anna J. Martin as the city clerk for the City of Mirada Hills. Before that first council could conduct any business, they had to have a city clerk.

That first meeting was unusual for several reasons. There was the immediate resignation of two council members, who had moved out of the area for business during the two years of waiting for incorporation. One councilman even came from Chicago to be sworn in and immediately resign to cover the legalities of the situation. The council had not planned on selecting a city treasurer right away since it had no money. However, city attorney Alex Googooian informed them they must have a treasurer—since that office was not listed on the program, they had to make their selection.

THAT FIRST CITY HALL

As the first city clerk of La Mirada, California, she brought her own card table, an old typewriter and boxes for files to set up the first office. This first city hall office was in an unfinished building at Valley View and Rosecrans. There was no ceiling, no carpet on the cement floor, no furniture or plumbing.

Even though that first council meeting lasted until 1:30 a.m., Ann opened the office at 8:00 a.m. Her first action was to get two telephones installed, but there were no desks to set them on, so they had to be placed on the floor.

The builders put up partitions around her while she was trying to conduct business on the phone. She had to go to the gas station to use the restroom. She even had to borrow money from the bank for her own salary the first few months because the city once again had no money.

That November, she had to handle her first election with no training. The measure up for vote was to change the name of the new city back to what the area had been called for years, La Mirada.

La Mirada's first city council, 1960. *Left to right*: Ann Martin (city clerk), Richard Danson (councilman), James Jenkins (councilman), Jerome Resnick (mayor, holding a framed gavel), Jack Clifford (councilman) and Estelle Troup (council Woman). *Courtesy of Gail Pearce from the La Mirada City Archives.*

City hall operated in that building for two years. She was city clerk for twenty-six years. In the first twenty-five years, she handled twelve elections and watched the city staff grow to 150.

Ann handled the city seal and signed all official documents along with the mayor. Her signature was on every piece of legislation passed by the city during those twenty-six years, including the official commendations the city presented to her.

She was the ultimate lady and always represented our city with poise, dignity and charm. She sparkled! While this job was more than she ever expected, she enjoyed the daily challenges and did not want to retire.

The word *clerk* doesn't sound like much; however, as city clerk, Ann provided the direct link from past to present to see that records and documents were preserved for posterity. She recorded all the city council meetings, and for those first few years, those meetings usually lasted until the wee hours of the mornings. She did so much, my mind boggles just trying to remember all the hats she wore.

Under that city clerk title, she was the registrar for voters, the election night tabulator, the proclamation preparer, the certificate preparer, the away meetings arranger, notary public and probably other jobs. Whatever needed doing, the refrain of each city council member was, "Don't worry, Ann will take care of it." The city work consumed her life.

Her Very Own Park

On June 19, 1987, Anna J. Martin and I happily posed together at the dedication of her park in the Hillsborough area of La Mirada. It is a lovely, quiet family park that she very humbly accepted as a great honor to have her name carved into the wooden park sign.

Sometimes she jokingly referred to herself as the "City Cluck"—the mother hen of this fair city.

While Wayne Grisham was congressman, he said Ann was the "unsung hero of City Hall" and gave her credit for working so hard to keep our city government running efficiently. Ann was a past president of the International Institute of Municipal Clerks. Her efficiency and expertise were known far and wide, even in Australia and Paris, France.

Early in January 1993, Ann suffered a stroke that paralyzed her right side. For the next nine years, her brilliant mind was locked up in a frustrating

The dedication of Anna J. Martin's new park in the Hillsborough area. Alice Palicz stands on the left and Anna J. Martin on the right. *Alice Palicz collection.*

quagmire. She could hear and understand but could not speak so we could understand her. At first, she was frustrated and could not understand when we did not know what she was trying to say. During those years we had some precious times as I visited regularly and took her and her caregiver out for various occasions.

LASTING MEMORIES

Sometimes when she was worn out, she felt alone and unappreciated. I gave my reply to that feeling at her memorial service on March 5, 2002. Thousands of people in La Mirada will always remember and love her.

14

JEROME O. OXMAN, FOUNDER OF OXMAN'S SURPLUS STORE, INTERVIEW

Conducted by Tony Aiello

The Tony Aiello Show *on AdviceRadio.com*
September 2, 2003
Transcribed by G.C.
Special Guest: Jerome "Jerry" Oxman and sitting in is Jerome's second son, Jason

TONY. And hello everybody, my name is Tony Aiello. Welcome to another edition of the *Tony Aiello Show*. You can check us out every Tuesday at five o'clock Pacific Time and today is September 2, 2003. We have a great program on for you. Join us in the next sixty minutes, for we have a wonderful in-studio guest.

Anybody that lives in La Mirada or who has lived in and around La Mirada the last ten, twenty, thirty, forty years, Mr. Jerome Oxman is here, along with his son Jason. Mr. Jerome Oxman, he is the owner and creator of the one and only Oxman's Surplus on Rosecrans and Valley View. All La Mirada citizens love Oxman's Surplus. It's just a great place to go to, even to this day, and Mr. Oxman, welcome to the program.

JERRY OXMAN. Well, thank you very much. I'm very happy to be here.

TONY. We appreciate you coming in here and giving us a behind-the-scenes look at Oxman's Surplus, which has been around since 1960?

JO. 1961, we started. Yes.

Tony. 1961, wow, that's a long time ago. In 1961, you almost started out with a garage?

JO. Yes, it was a garage-type building, and we had nothing in that garage to start with and so we made up display tables with pallets and we covered it with material and we had quite a bit of units that I had bid on previously to that point where I opened up the store. And we just filled it up with a lot of gadgets and so on and that was the beginning.

Tony. That was the beginning of it all, wow. What happened next to bring it up to the next level after you started out in a garage?

JO. We started bidding on government equipment, and the very first one that I bid on was hydraulic. We used to carry quite a bit of hydraulics. In that time, the fellows were lowering and raising their automobiles. If you remember driving down the street and the car would rise up about two feet and back down again, so we used to sell the hydraulics for that reason. And one lot that I bid on was three hundred cans of what I thought was water, but it turned out when I bid on it—well I won the bid, because I only paid ten cents apiece for the cans, but there was hydraulics in that lot and so I won the lot and when I arrived home, why there was a letter waiting for me offering me four hundred dollars for the cans, so I figured that there was something wrong there. I took one of the cans over to a company called Handy and Harmon; they were assayers for precious metals. We found out that there were eight of silver in each can, so for ten cents I bought quite a bit of beer.

Tony. A good find, that's for sure. You mentioned the bidding on government items. For people that don't know, that's the definition of surplus. You actually bid on items that the government doesn't want anymore?

JO. Yes, that's true, they demilitarize it, and we received invitations to bid from all over the country, and I have a million and a half miles under my belt just traveling and inspecting government equipment. And that's how they do it, they send us invitations to bid and we have to hop a plane and go to the city that is involved and inspect the items, and we put a bid in as to what we think we can sell it for.

Tony. Do you still actively do that to this day?

JO. Yes we do, we do it locally now from Boeing to North American.

Tony. Does Jason help out with your other son, Murray?

JO. Yes, Jason has quite a bit of experience. He bid a lot in El Toro, California, also.

Tony. Oh, wow.

JO. He bought ejection seats there.

TONY. So, military items must be a hot commodity with all of the wars going on. They must have been a hot commodity in the Gulf War, but I'm thinking back now. We didn't have many wars going on in the eighties, so that must have been kind of a slow time. When there are wars, which are never a good thing, do sales go up? Is it like that at Oxman's, people coming in for military items, camouflage clothing and all of that?

JO. Yes, all the time. And of course even back in the eighties, the government had so much equipment in their warehouses, that they would release it constantly and that's why we were able to buy items that were set up by the government all the time. And sometimes we could buy it for just pennies on the dollar, but now it's a little different story. We have to pay through the nose to buy it, because there is a shortage of military equipment, good sellable equipment that the public would like to buy.

TONY. Is there a lot of competition in the business now compared to thirty or forty years ago?

JO. Yes, we have over two hundred people bidding against us, so that's competition, and you have to know what you're doing and according to what you think you can sell the material for. You have to be very careful.

TONY. I should mention that Mr. Oxman has been very involved in the community. For many years when I played La Mirada Little League [I remember] seeing certain teams that had their little patches on their backs sponsored by Oxman's Surplus. He's sponsored La Mirada Little League for many years. He is past president of the La Mirada Chamber of Commerce. Past president of Meals on Wheels, now that program is still going strong.

JO. Yes it is.

TONY. Tell us a little about the Saturn engine story, because I know you told me that story the last time we met, and you were quite proud of that. Can you tell us a little about that? You were involved with the country of Japan?

JO. I bid on two Saturn engines. They're twenty-million-dollar engines, by the way.

TONY. And this was in what year?

JO. This is about twenty years ago. When I first saw the engines, they were brand-new and beautiful, and I said to myself, I just have to have those engines, and so I bid quite high. As a matter of fact, I bid in the thousands, and the bid wasn't going to be opening until the following weekend, and so I went back home and I started thinking, and I thought to myself, my God, I just put too much money into that. So I went back and I withdrew my bid before it opened, and I cut the bid in half, and when it opened, why I was fifty-eight cents higher than the next bidder, so I won both Saturn engines.

Tony. By fifty-eight cents each?

JO. Yes.

Tony. Explain what the Saturn engine is to our listeners?

JO. It's called a J-2 engine, and that is the second stage of the Saturn that put the men on the moon.

Tony. Wow!

JO. Yes and there was two engines in each unit, and the main engines, I believe, was the F-1 and these engines went up with the astronauts to the moon and they ejected onto the moon and got onto the moon itself, with the help of those two engines.

Tony. The actual engines?

JO. Yes, they were the actual engines. We had them for about eight to ten years, displayed them in our store, and then one day a Japanese gentleman came in and said they understood that we have Saturn engines, and I said, "Yes we do," and he said, "We'd like to have one of them. We'd like to lease one of them to put in our Space Park," and I said, "Well instead of you leasing it, why don't you bring our family to Japan?" And he said, "That might be a good idea." It took about two weeks, and I figured, well, that was shot down. He came back and said, "We're ready to go, and we want the engine right away." We arranged for shipment and that was it. He took that one engine, and the next two months we were in Japan with my wife and then the boys went after that.

Tony. So he wanted the engine that bad?

JO. Oh, yes.

Tony. Memorabilia in Japan—that was a hot item?

JO. Yes, Japan was much more excited about the journey to the moon than America was.

Tony. Did he end up with both of them?

JO. Yes, we finally sold both of them to Japan. That was a very nice situation.

Tony. Really—a fascinating story. At what point did Oxman's turn into a retail store?

JO. Strictly retail.

Tony. What determined that decision?

JO. Well, I've been in the retail business working for someone before, and I just decided you work for a person for ten years and they've promised things and they never come through, so I just decided to leave and open my own business. We started in with military equipment, mostly hydraulics and so on. We had about forty to fifty thousand pounds of hydraulic cylinders that I had purchased previously. And so we started selling that sort of thing, and then we had little items that people liked. We added all kinds of equipment, and that went on for quite some time. Jason here was just born at that time. I had to run from the store to attend his birth, but that's how we started.

TONY. Was that right about the time you moved into the building you're in now?

JO. No, the big building was about a year before, and of course that was the Big A. I leased that from Big A.

TONY. Everybody remembers Big A and Unimart and Disco Faire.

JO. And then we finally purchased the whole complex.

TONY. You used to do some advertising. I remember on cable TV in the late eighties, and early nineties?

JO. We were on channel 4 and channel 7, but we haven't been advertising too much lately, but we're going to start shortly, yes, and maybe with you too?

TONY. We'll see what happens with that. Your wife, Miriam, she's very much involved?

JO. Yes, she was very instrumental in my starting, and she's been very helpful all through the years, and when we had two children, why, she would bring them down in cribs and she'd work with me during the day. Yes, she did a good job.

TONY. Tell me about in your early days, your mail-order business. Isn't that something that catapulted you?

JO. Yes, we started that, and we were selling aircraft instruments, mostly through the mail. It's not like it is now.

TONY. Well, nothing is.

JO. But I did have a source of aircraft instruments through a gentleman, and he would allow me to use his inventory, so we advertised all through the country for aircraft instruments and we did very well, and that's how we started with that. That was even before we opened the store. We had one deal where one man wanted one item that we advertised, and through that item, we sold a large quantity and that started us out well, so we were lucky in that area also.

TONY. Let's talk a little about what you can expect when you walk into Oxman's today? One of the great things about Oxman's that still attracts the kids is the unique items you have—rare items. You have cockpits there, actual cockpits from jet aircraft and that sort of thing. You also have a thing called "gadgeteers paradise." Is that still in existence?

JO. Yes it is.

TONY. Describe some of the unusual things that nobody else in LA County can say they have?

JO. Well, you're talking about the cockpit, that's a B-17 Bomber and that was found in the Sahara Desert. It was buried for thirty years.

Tony. No way?

JO. Yes, it crash-landed, and the men just didn't get out of the aircraft in time. It was too hot, and they were injured and they died in the aircraft. The winds covered the plane, and it was covered for thirty years, and finally, it was uncovered by an archaeological group.

TONY. In what year?

JO. This was about fifteen years ago [1988]. They found it and they brought it to me.

TONY. Because? Why did they bring it to you?

JO. They had heard about me.

TONY. Oh, wow!

JO. And they figured I might want it, because it was an unusual thing.

TONY. So you're that well known in the surplus world?

JO. Yes, I have managed to become very well known.

TONY. A Southern California icon we have here.

JO. So I purchased it from them.

TONY. And it's still there today?

JO. It's still there, Tony. We are going to place the B-17 cockpit in the very front of the store as part of our museum.

TONY. What are some of the other items that you can brag about that you have there?

JO. We have a Bull Putt missile, which weighs about five thousand pounds, and two of them are carried under the F-100 Fighter Bomber and that's in our yard. We also have the original Ranger engine that every pilot who joined the service trained with. As a matter of fact, one of the planes had the engine crash into one of our barracks. And we have a one-hundred-year-old whaling cannon. An original whaling cannon, all brass.

TONY. Do you have World War I items?

JO. Yes, we have a few World War I items.

TONY. What are some of your oldest?

JO. In one of our cases, we have where one man received five Purple Hearts. He was wounded five times and came out of it alright. That whole case is filled with all kinds of memorabilia, medals and daggers and swords and so on.

TONY. Mr. Oxman, how many visits do you get from veterans? Do a lot of guys come in and look around?

JO. Yes, we have a lot of that. A lot of them are veterans, and they're enthralled. If they had a very good experience, it brings back all kinds of memories, and pilots come in and get up into the B-17 and just sit there. They amuse themselves with the controls and go back in their memory. They seem to enjoy that quite a bit.

TONY. Actually some fascinating stories of how Oxman's got started. I don't even think that a lot of people that live around here who have visited Oxman's know all this stuff, and we're so happy to inform everybody on the story behind Oxman's Surplus. You must have endless stories such as these?

JO. Yes, I could go on for three or four of these. Maybe even weeks.

TONY. What are some of your more popular items today in 2003?

JO. I think the most popular are the military clothing. We have all different types of clothing that they used in the service. We also have boots from the service and so on.

TONY. It all started out in 1961, and here we are forty-two years later and still going strong. What does the future hold for Oxman's now? Are you guys all into it? Are you going to carry on the tradition?

JO. "Yes, my two sons, Murray and Jason. Jason is very adept at knowing how to purchase surplus. He's good on his own, so there's no problem there. Both Murray and Jason are good at purchasing the merchandise. So they have the future in front of them.

TONY. I have to tell you, I love these stories, seeing family businesses grow and prosper, and I love seeing obviously the closeness that you guys have and how much you all have a passion for this, and it's really uplifting to me, and I hope that's coming across to our listeners.

JO. Well, the comments from our customers are. "We still love this store, after all of these years."

TONY. I'm glad to know that you have no intention of ever leaving in the near future, because people are really into that kind of nostalgia and they're used to seeing familiar buildings and landmarks around them and a lot of people don't like change, and I think as long as Oxman's and other establishments stay in our lives, it gives us a feeling of being comfortable in our own community. I'm glad you guys told us you're sticking around and not going anywhere, and I really appreciate you gentlemen coming in this evening and letting us know about the story behind Oxman's Surplus. It has truly been a pleasure having you in.

JO. The pleasure was all ours, Tony.

TONY. A thank-you to you fine gentleman. That wraps up today's show. I want to say thank you to everyone who was listening out there.

15

FOREIGN DAIRY FARMERS FOUND A HOME IN CALIFORNIA

From the Desert Sun, *1978*

They came from Holland, Portugal and Switzerland. They were dairymen in their home countries and they came to Southern California, where the climate was mild and there was plenty of reasonable-priced, level land for them to reestablish their family dairies.

Around the turn of the century, the center of dairy activity was San Pedro and Torrance and then it spread eastward to Artesia, Bellflower, Cerritos, Anaheim, La Mirada, La Palma and a place called Hynes that later was changed to Paramount.

Some of the more adventurous dairy families ventured to more remote corners of the area: El Monte, West Covina, and Azusa and even to the Chino Valley 50 miles east of the Los Angeles basin. But the dairy cow capital of the Southern California area was the region from the coast east to Anaheim. Between 1910 and 1945, hundreds of dairies were established here.

"Dad and Mother packed all of the seven kids here from Holland in 1930 and we started a dairy in El Monte," La Mirada dairyman Cor Van Dam told the Council of California Growers.

"In 1944, I went into the business myself and moved down here in 1952. It was a community of dairies then, with some olive trees, citrus and dry farming mixed in," he said.

"The major attraction of the area was the climate," Van Dam explained. "Because it's relatively close to the ocean, for we experienced the cool ocean breezes, a bit of fog and mild temperatures most of the time. Cows like that kind of weather and therefore, give more milk."

"La Mirada and all the surrounding communities were small. I don't think there were more than 20 families around here in the early 1950s. It was a rural area, and the massive urbanization you see today had not yet begun," Van Dam said.

Toward the middle of the 1950s, one of the pioneer ranches in the area, owned by the McNally family, was sold and subdivided. "Until then, I really couldn't see it coming," Van Dam said. "Our move from El Monte was prompted by the beginnings of urban encroachment and I should have known it would happen here too."

"From 1955 to 1965," according to Van Dam, "one dairy after another was replaced by warehouses, shopping centers, housing and apartment developments and freeways.

"There are less than a half-dozen dairies remaining in Los Angeles County. Most of them will be sold and the dairies would have moved to friendlier—and more economically feasible areas."

Van Dam plans to stay, but he has reservations. "I know this isn't dairy country anymore, but I just want to hold cut awhile longer and do business and serve the community, because I like the people who live here."

16

COR VAN DAM, FOUNDER OF VALLEY VIEW FARMS DAIRY, INTERVIEW

AdviceRadio.com 2005, The *Tony Aiello Show*

Special Guest: Cor Van Dam
Transcribed directly from the show by G.C.

Tony. My name is Tony Aiello and you are listening to AdviceRadio.com, and I have the pleasure to be sitting with Cor Van Dam of Valley View Farms. He's probably the most successful businessman I think in the history of La Mirada, if you think about it, and he has taken his time to sit with us on this morning here and he says he is happy to be with us. Mr. Van Dam how are you doing today?

Cor Van Dam. Today is one of the most beautiful days in my life.

Tony. Well I'm glad to hear that. I guess we picked a good day for you to stop by?

Cor. I'm retired, and I'm enjoying myself very much.

Tony. "Good, we're glad to hear that. I know a lot of listeners are excited about hearing from you, because you know since the dairy closed here in town, we just hadn't had a chance to see you as much, and we appreciate you taking the time with us today. The dairy debuted in 1953 in January thereabouts, right?

Cor. That's when we opened our Cash N' Carry facilities; however, we moved the dairy here in 1951. We bought the property in 1950, and it was 1951 when we built the facilities, and we opened our Cash N' Carry on January 15, 1953.

Tony. Yes, the Cash N' Carry, that's the little market everybody went to who were brand-new residents here in close proximity.

Cor. That's the market exactly, and one of the reasons why we opened the Cash N' Carry, is because we noticed that the area across the street, across Valley View from us, the McNally Ranch was sold and was being developed into residential tracts. We thought this would be a good time for us to explore the selling of our milk via Cash N' Carry, in which it worked out very well.

Tony. That was a great idea for you back when.

Cor. An extremely favorable idea, Tony.

Tony. So you watched the homes rise. That's where Pep Boys is currently, and those homes right behind Pep Boys and where Pep Boys is, it used to be a Market Basket, so, as the builders arrived, you decided to take advantage of the opportunity?

Cor. That's correct, but let me first open, of course, by saying there was no Market Basket.

Tony. Right, it was before 1953.

Cor. There was just vacant property, but the area east of Market Basket, the property was being developed into residential homes, and that was part of the McNally Ranch. When we first moved here of course, there were no homes. It was just still a ranch and where they had the olive groves and some orange groves to the east of us. Why, to the north of us, there was, which the Foster Park area is now, there were large alfalfa fields and a small pond.

Tony. That's right, where I grew up. So you saw all that change over the years? Let's back up a little bit, why did you decide to come out? You didn't live in California your whole life, obviously, you came from?

Cor. We moved here in 1930, as immigrants from the Netherlands.

Tony. That is awesome Cor.

Cor. With Dad and Mother and seven children, and they permitted us to locate in Southern California. It was to my dad's way of thinking, it would be better for the family to grow up in the United States in California, and thousands of people left and experienced the same thing and to this day we are thankful for the people of the United States who permitted us to make a living here in California. It's been nothing but joy living in the United States and for our family, our whole family.

TONY. The American Dream, you work hard you can pretty much achieve anything?

COR. Yes, thank the heavens for that.

TONY. Was it your father or was it you that decided on the dairy industry?

COR. My dad was absorbed in dairy farming in the Netherlands.

TONY. Okay, there's the connection.

COR. So coming over here, it was just natural, and he was very successful in doing it over there working hard like you mentioned.

TONY. That's where you got it from?

COR. There's nothing wrong with that. Now before we moved to La Mirada, I had a dairy, several dairies in El Monte at one time, but it was becoming crowded with the industrial parks coming into being, so we decided to move out in the country and that's one reason we made a purchase here in La Mirada, which was Norwalk at that time. So, when my wife and I first married—

TONY. Your wife, Florence?

COR. My wife, Florence, and incidentally in another two months, we'll celebrate our sixtieth wedding anniversary.

TONY. Oh my, congratulations, that is unbelievable.

COR. We lived in El Monte, and then, since I mentioned that it was getting overcrowded, we decided to move to La Mirada—Norwalk. It was a rather expensive move. The property cost higher, but we decided to do it anyway, and it's been very successful.

TONY. So you picked out a piece of land to operate your dairy on and—

COR. Yes, we wanted a piece of ground at the proper slope and the proper conditions to build a dairy and so on, and we found this acreage here.

TONY. On Rosecrans and Valley View?

COR. Yes, Rosecrans and Valley View, we found it very much to our liking, and it was an exciting time for both Florence and I to be able to build a dairy, and building a dairy at that time was a state-of-the-art operation, a large dairy as it was in those days, and we had so many people come out and visit our place, which at that time was a wholesale operation, and it was just a tremendous experience for a person starting out the business and to be able to build a brand new place to our liking. It's been successful ever since.

TONY. That was around 1953?

COR. That was all in 1950, when we purchased the property. We built the dairy in 1951.

TONY. Mr. Cor Van Dam, owner and operator of Valley View Farms, is with us, and he has been the owner close to fifty years, right, Cor?

COR. I would say probably closer to fifty years.

TONY. Cor keeps on telling me that we are just common ordinary folks, and I agree with that, but there are a lot of people interested in your life, and that's why we are here today. We both recently attended the city of La Mirada's forty-fifth anniversary celebration, and we were talking about the time machine they had set up there where they had a bunch of historical memorabilia, and I was looking in one of the books. Do you remember the Polley's Blue Book they use to have in the city of La Mirada? They used to have that directory. They had the first issue there on display. I think it debuted in 1951 or '52, and you had your advertisements up on the top page, the Valley View Farm ads in the directory, the city of La Mirada's first directory. I can remember all the way up to when they stopped printing the Blue Book. Did you used to have your advertisements in the directory the entire time?

COR. As far as I can remember, yes, we had the first colored page inside of the front cover.

TONY. I remember growing up seeing that every four pages at the top, it said, "Valley View Farms." Right from the beginning you were already advertising in La Mirada.

COR. Some of the other advertising we did was in the La Mirada Theater, the Stanley Warner Theater, which at the time was during the show inside. The Blue Book ads were well received, because it was part of La Mirada.

TONY. The dairy was pretty much successful from the very beginning, correct?

COR. Yes, indeed it was, Tony.

TONY. All the way through the 1950s and in the early 1960s and the late '60s?

COR. You know, it just seemed to me that when we first opened, the years when people just moved into La Mirada, so many people were strangers even to Southern California, and we became a place for them to meet each other and to visit, and we always had people come through and visit our place. It was a time of growing, not only for us as Valley View Farms but also for the community. It was a growing process and people were strangers and they wanted to get acquainted with one another.

TONY. Everybody was growing together back in the beginning.

Students are taking part in extracting and receiving Cor Van Dam's milk pasteurization product, 1964. *Courtesy of Gail Pearce from the La Mirada City Archives.*

COR. They really were, and it was a place to meet each other and we had so many people stop by, and we could feel that they wanted to get to know you, and they wanted to become familiar with the neighbors, and so I personally would go out into the community and talk to people, when they first moved in, and to welcome them to La Mirada.

TONY. Wow that is something, Cor.

COR. We wanted to become personally acquainted with the neighbors. It was just a good feeling you had. It was a community effort and a concerted effort on the part of so many people.

TONY. And you know the roots of those times still remain today, because La Mirada in many ways has grown into a place where you can feel that you're in a community. The city itself should be very proud of itself for what has transpired over the years, becoming incorporated in 1960.

COR. Yes, for sure.

TONY. And that we recently celebrated the anniversary. You've been pretty much involved with the city itself?

COR. Yes, even though we were not in the city limits.

TONY. Technically, yes. We should explain that. The area that Valley View Farms sits on is actually considered the Foster Park area of La Mirada, if you want to get technical, and that did not get annexed into the city until 1978, which was a very controversial action in the city then. So, actually where the dairy sits was not part of the city until 1977, 1978?

COR. That's correct, sir.

TONY. So technically it was county land, but the address read La Mirada and we all knew [it] was La Mirada.

COR. Our allegiance was always towards the city of La Mirada.

TONY. Well that's the case with most of the residents west of Valley View. Our allegiance too has always been towards the city of La Mirada. It just took them a little time to get to us, but returning to what we were talking about Cor, you were involved with the city?

COR. Yes we were involved. We supported the chamber of commerce, the Rotary Club, which we're still members [of] and also Little Leagues.

TONY. When did a lot of people recognize you for what took place on the Little League field, which I played on myself, and when did La Mirada Little League start playing on your cow pasture?"

COR. I would say the late 1960s. Various Little Leagues played at the Catholic school.

TONY. Yes, St. Paul of the Cross."

COR. Yes, that's right, St. Paul of the Cross needed the land then for development, and they approached me asking, "if I had an area, a little parcel of land in the back and if they could use it" and I said, "Sure, but I expect to collect some rent."

St. Paul of the Cross Catholic Church, which opened in 1957. *Courtesy of Loren Penner from Discover La Mirada.*

Tony. So you came up with an exclusive agreement?

Cor. Yes, and that was one dollar a year.

Tony. One dollar per year?

Cor. And they paid it religiously. On every opening day.

Tony. Yes, you would walk out there every opening day, every March, and they would give you your one dollar. And this community would be thanking you because you provided that land for kids and others, including myself to play baseball on it, and it was named Van Dam Stadium. It remained there for many years, and I always told everybody, "I always knew when it was summer, because you could hear the PA announcer on the speakers," and I lived relatively close and those were truly wonderful days. In the 1970s, my mom always used to send me on my bike to get milk or bread or whatever we needed to the Cash N' Carry back and forth to Valley View Farms, just great memories.

Tony. I'm sitting with Mr. Cor Van Dam of Valley View Farms. Cor, right now we're sitting in I guess your business office. Let me ask you, when you first moved out here, you didn't live in the house you live in now, there was actually another house built back there when you bought the land back then, right, Cor?

Cor. Yes Tony, when we first moved here, there was a house, as a matter of fact, there were two houses on the place, and one was facing Valley View and there was one house that was set off facing Rosecrans in the back of this property. We lived there, Florence and I and our family for three years, and then we built the house where we live in now."

Tony. And there was a little road leading up to that house off of Rosecrans?

Cor. That is correct, you remember that?

Tony. I saw a few aerial pictures of this entire area, Cor. So in the 1970s now, was there ever a down time for your business?

Cor. No, and there's no such thing as a day off when you're in the dairy business. We gradually increased our herd from 250 head of cattle in El Monte. We built that up to 600 in La Mirada. That was as many cows as we could have at the place. They were crowded at that time. That's another reason we decided to move our herd up to Idaho in the late 1990s.

Tony. Besides when the dairy was at full capacity and operating besides the Cash N' Carry, where else did you distribute your milk to?

Cor. We had some school contracts, Norwalk–La Mirada school Districts, and we sold a lot of milk through the schools, but we had no other outlet except our Cash N' Carry.

Tony. Really, so you must have pushed a lot of milk through that Cash N' Carry over the years?

Cor. Remember, we had quite a few schools in La Mirada and Norwalk, which we personally delivered to. But yes, Tony, we did a lot of business at the Cash N' Carry. It was probably one of the most successful Cash N' Carrys in the Southland.

Tony. Did you innovate the drive-through concept?

Cor. We were not the first Cash N' Carry operation, but we were pretty much in the beginning of the Cash N' Carry trend, which has slowed down considerably now, since it's so convenient to buy milk in cartons in the grocery store.

Tony. Back in the '40s and '50s when automobiles were starting to become affordable, were the A&Ws and Cash N' Carry's trying to accommodate?

Cor. There was a time when home delivery was popular, and as you said, when people were starting to become more mobile, they would just get in their cars.

Tony. So once again, you took advantage of that and became very successful and that continued into the 1980s? That must have consumed a lot of your time. I know you had special people helping you along the way, but it must have been almost a twenty-four-hour job running your own business?

Cor. When you mentioned help, I probably was one of the most fortunate dairy operators in Southern California with the kind of help I had, not just help as far as the dairy operation is concerned, but I was very, very successful to get young people to work out there at the dairy. They enjoyed it, and we enjoyed having them. Good young people. They made our operations as successful as it has been.

Tony. Then you had your staff, your farmhands, people don't realize it, it's like running a farm isn't it, Cor?

Cor. Yes, to this day, I wished I had another hundred acres, where I could hire young people and get them out and do some work, rather than what they shouldn't be doing, but it's a new area and it's an altogether different world and they got to make the best of it. I'm sure that La Mirada is still well equipped with young people like we had in those days.

Tony. Well, so we continued through the '80s. When did you decide that you might want to start beginning to look at selling the cattle? When did that idea first come about?"

Cor. I have four daughters, but only one son. My son graduated from college and always worked on the dairy in his spare time.

Tony. And his name is—?

Cor. Cornel. He wanted to continue operating the dairy, but not the Cash N' Carry, the dairy cattle.

Tony. Not the retail part?

Cor. That's right, he wanted to expand, and Valley View Farms was not large enough for expansion, so we decided to move elsewhere and found some property, several hundred acres in Idaho. So we moved our dairy herd to Idaho, which was a good move, and we increased the herd to three to four thousand head of cattle. Cornel, my son, did the operating of the farm, the dairy farm, and that brought us to the point of developing the property. And that was in the middle 1990s.

Tony. Did anybody try to deter you from that, or did anyone approach you from the community to ask you to stay or perhaps express an opinion?

Cor. I'm glad you asked that question. We know of some dairy operations and dairy farms that are not welcomed in their community. We never had that problem. The city of La Mirada was always very good to us, willing to cooperate in whatever we wanted and therefore we felt very akin to the city of La Mirada."

Tony. So, the closing of the dairy was very sad for a lot of us.

Cor. It was a sad day for me. After you build something that's successful and then you see it change to something else. The cattle was always my expertise and my livelihood and I enjoyed it, and to have that removed, it takes a little while to get used to. There's still good people living here in La Mirada, and we're still living here and we love La Mirada.

Tony. Oh, we love the fact that you're living here—we don't ever want you to move. I bet now when you look around, you never could have imagined what you see now in the way of businesses, being that you moved here in 1950, and what has transpired over the last fifty-five years?

Cor. Yes, it's almost unbelievable. When we first moved here there were farms, dairy farms, vegetable farms, flower farms, et cetera. We feel ourselves very fortunate to have raised our family here. Five children and they've all attended local schools here and all attended college. They too were happy living here, and they've expressed that many, many times and here on the dairy."

Tony. That's great, what else could you ask for?

Cor. That's the best of everything."

Tony. Yes it is. It's the American Dream to its fullest. You served on the planning commission?

Cor. Quite a long time, Tony.

Tony. What was that experience like?

Cor. Very interesting Tony, it was an experience for me because it entitled me to look at properties that the city wanted to develop, and we were entitled to investigate situations and make adjustments as well as judgments later on it. It was all tremendous experience. It was brilliant, and to this day, I want you and people to know that you got to give God the glory for all these things. He's been so good to us. And Tony, let me mention this to you. It's wonderful that we have young people like yourself living here in La Mirada and working here in La Mirada."

Tony. Well, thank you, Cor.

Cor. And you're upholding the city as well. You become part of it, and that's extremely important and I appreciate it. Thank you."

Tony. You're very welcome. I'm trying to keep as many memories alive and keep the city going in a positive direction and uphold a lot of our traditions here and doing my part.

Cor. You're certainly doing that.

Tony. Thank you so much.

Cor. Beautiful job, Tony.

Tony. Is there anything you wanted to mention? How are you feeling these days?

Cor. Our children are all happily married and living in communities where they are in turn working, and that is very satisfying as far as I'm concerned.

Tony. You mentioned your son, now does he continue to this day to farm in Idaho? Now the original La Mirada herd is still in Idaho?"

Cor. Actually, Tony, the herd has been sold and my son is now engaged in real estate over in the Boise area.

Tony. I see.

Cor. We still think about the animals and read our magazines. Florence and I are very happy and consider ourselves very fortunate living here in La Mirada and meeting people like yourself and many others.

Tony. I want to thank you, Cor, for taking this time sitting down with me and my listeners and granting us this interview. Thank you very much for this time.

Cor. Tony, thank you, and I wish you a lot of success.

Tony. Thank you.

Cor. The pleasure is all mine, Tony

Tony. Thanks again, Cor.

17
CHANGING AND CONCERNING TIMES

The worst storm in La Mirada's history slammed into the community in December 1982, downing hundreds of trees. Other events of the 1980s included the distribution of surplus, cheese and butter by the federal government. In February 1983 and again in March 1984, hundreds of senior citizens and low-income residents lined up at the La Mirada Mall to receive their allocations. In an attempt to reduce the risk of kidnapping, eight thousand youngsters were fingerprinted in "Operation Kid print" sponsored in the fall of 1983 by local PTAs and the Los Angeles County Sheriff's Department. Strong storms in the spring of 1983 damaged some of the city's horse trails, resulting in their closure until repairs could be made. Just before the Olympic Games opened in Los Angeles in the summer of 1984, runners bearing the Olympic torch made their way through La Mirada.

Looking at additional issues in the community, one finds concern in the 1960s over speeding trains and speeding cars. Trains passed through La Mirada in 1960 at speeds of up to ninety miles per hour. The city was successful at getting that reduced to a maximum of sixty miles per hour. Valley View had a speed limit of sixty-five until 1961, when the city and county agreed on a forty-five miles-per-hour posting. Teenage drinking at Gardenhill Park became an issue in 1964, and local residents petitioned the city to crack down on the situation. In 1965, the city council first began to deal with the issue of controlling entertainment in the city's bars. The adequacy of police protection through the Los Angeles County Sheriff's

Department was debated nearly from the outset of cityhood. While serious crime in La Mirada has been lower overall than in most surrounding communities, the number of burglaries in the community has been a major problem since the 1960s. Car stereos were a main target of thefts in the 1960s. Drug abuse problems became a major community concern by the late 1960s. To improve police and hopefully serve as a deterrent to criminal activity, Sheriff's Department helicopters began patrolling La Mirada in 1968. In 1969, there was considerable controversy over a proposed extension of Knott Avenue into a major La Mirada thoroughfare. The city council decided against this plan in 1969.

One of the issues of the early 1970s was the use of the open fields in undeveloped north La Mirada by dirt bikers. While the hills were ideal from a cyclist's perspective, the noise was a nuisance to nearby residents. The city council passed an ordinance in June 1970 banning motorcycles on the city's undeveloped property. Because of continued violations of this ordinance, the city brought mounted sheriff's deputies to patrol the city's hills in 1971. Crime continued to be a major issue in the 1970s, with burglaries and drug-related crimes all too common. Over 400 bicycles were stolen in the city in 1970. Car stereos and tools continued to be among the most frequently stolen items in the early 1970s, surpassed by television sets, home stereos and microwave ovens in the late 1970s. In February 1977, Scorpion Jewelers at the La Mirada Mall lost $45,000 worth of merchandise in a major jewel heist. In addition to theft, vandalism of local schools and churches was a problem during the 1970s as well as the 1980s. In spite of these problems, La Mirada's crime rate compared very favorably to other Southland cities. The summary of criminal activity in La Mirada for 1980 showed no murders, 17 cases of rape, 53 robberies, 170 aggravated assaults, 823 burglaries, 788 cases of larceny and theft and 177 auto thefts. When it came to traffic fatalities, La Mirada consistently maintained a good record of safety.

The city became increasingly concerned over the fate of La Mirada's olive trees in the 1970s. Many residents were uprooting or drastically trimming trees that were once a part of the McNally Ranch's olive groves because of the purple mess created by fallen olives. The city published a brochure on olive trees in 1971 in an attempt to persuade homeowners to spare the trees. In the mid-1970s, the city began a program of spraying the trees to prevent olives from forming. One grove of olive trees remains from the McNally era, located on a corner of the Biola University campus between the La Mirada Creek and La Mirada Boulevard.

A pristine sheriff's vehicle attracts a crowd of youngster's during a function at Regional Park, circa 2000s. *Courtesy of Loren Penner from Discover La Mirada.*

Among the controversial issues of the 1970s was the placing of an Easter display on the Rosecrans Avenue median, which triggered a verbal conflict over the appropriateness of a religious display on public property.

La Mirada's battle with vice and pornography dates to at least 1971 when the Bull Pen closed down after annexation of that area into the city in 1974. Another challenge faced by the city in this regard was an adult bookstore proposed on Alondra Boulevard in 1979. By various tactics, the city delayed the opening of the store and then passed an emergency ordinance aimed at keeping sex-oriented shops and bookstores out of the community. Owners of the bookstore sued the city for $1 million in November 1979, and the following month a court order restrained La Mirada from enforcing its emergency ordinance. In early 1980, over six hundred residents packed the council chambers and lobby of city hall for a public hearing concerning the bookstore. A citizens' group was formed to take appropriate action to discourage the proposed new business, and the whole enterprise failed to materialize when the bookstore lost its lease. Another problem for the city began in 1980 with the appearance of "exotic male dancers" at Jimmy's Rendezvous, a restaurant at the La Mirada Mall. The establishment underwent ownership and name changes, but the city continued to be concerned that a nightclub was forming where a restaurant belonged. Permission was denied for male strip shows in July 1981, and the establishment lost its dance permit in late 1983.

Another controversial issue faced by the city was the matter of banning smoking in certain public places. The business community was asked for input from the city council and had mixed feelings about the proposed ordinance. In June 1976, the city council approved an ordinance banning smoking in a number of designated public areas and set fines of ten to fifty dollars for violations. In another controversial move, the city council voted to end the annual July Fourth picnic and fireworks show after the 1978 event was marred by drinking, firecrackers, fires, excessive littering and a rock and bottle throwing fracas in which twenty-one persons were arrested. Gang activity in parts of the city has been of concern for years, and in 1980, a group known as United Parents of La Mirada formed to combat the problem.

La Mirada has not been without problems, but the city's citizens and government have faced them and dealt with them in effective ways.

La Mirada 1985

It would be interesting to see Andrew McNally's reaction to the La Mirada of 1985 if he were able to see it nearly a century after he purchased this area and dreamed of his "gentlemen's estates." He would no doubt be amazed to know that in 1985, 41,000 people lived here in an incorporated city of 7.78 square miles, 19 miles from the center of what is now the second-largest city in the United States. He would also be astounded to learn that his former ranch lands were now developed with an assessed valuation of nearly $1.1 billion. The existence of 12,500 dwelling units in La Mirada selling for between $85,000 and $350,000 would probably come as quite a surprise to McNally. One of the more popular family restaurants, which opened way back in 1933, was the Carriage Restaurant, and in 1985, the restaurant has stood there attracting community folks for fifty-two years. The Carriage Restaurant would be torn down and replaced by a McDonald's in 2014.

As La Mirada celebrated twenty-five years of cityhood, its residents could look back with pride on what had been accomplished in a relatively short time. Careful planning and zoning since incorporation resulted in an aesthetically pleasing and well-balanced community, essentially residential

Left: Eighty-one years of serving La Mirada residents. The menu for La Mirada's classic Carriage Restaurant, in business since 1933. *Glen Cantrell, the one of two Authors' collection.*

Below: Police onlookers watch La Mirada mayor and city councilmen equally, taking part in being silly, wearing firefighter suits at Biola University's grounds, early 1990s. *Dr. David Peters collection.*

in character but with an active and attractive industrial sector as well as conveniently located shopping facilities.

Most residents maintained high standards of upkeep on their property, and the city had an aggressive policy of landscaping and maintenance of city-owned property, including parkways and medians. But a community is more than land and buildings. It is people who have made La Mirada a pleasant and, in many respects, an ideal community in which to live and raise families

While so much has been accomplished, there is yet room for creativity, growth and innovation. We must maintain that which is good in our community and strive to make the good even better. We have seen a marvelous foundation laid. May the years ahead be as successful in producing the good life for those who will make La Mirada their home. In fact, there were comical times to be had.

PART II

1

MOVING ONWARD THROUGH TIME

1953

By Alice Palicz

We built our home in 1953 on Tricia Lane, the first street curbed and guttered and dedicated to the County of Los Angeles in the south part of La Mirada near Alondra and Stage Roads. We were in an abandoned orange grove. The trees were dying, and the fruit was shriveled up and browning. The oranges did not look inviting at all, but they were the sweetest oranges we had ever eaten. We learned that the reason for this was that they were truly tree ripened.

We removed ten orange trees to build our 1582-square-foot home plus a two-and-a-half car detached garage. To save the remaining trees, we hauled hoses that we hooked up to the meter at the curb and strung 180 feet, the length of our lot. We provided our friends with fresh orange juice until all those old oranges were gone. We could not waste them.

In our construction, we used lathe and plaster with hardwood flooring on a raised foundation, complete with a bath and three-quarters. We were really living!

From the rear of our lot we could see Catalina Island and later watched strange-looking creations on flatbed trucks parading down Firestone Boulevard to the new theme park called Disneyland. Much of Disneyland was built in Burbank and then trucked to Anaheim. What fun it was to view these processions with wonderment as to what that was going to be.

Emil, my husband, was in the first survey crew for the new development. The survey office was in an old house situated roughly between the Neff

Barn and the George House near the corner of San Cristobal and San Esteban next to present-day Neff Park.

He located the dam of what had been Windermere Lake at roughly Rosecrans and Biola Avenues. Andrew McNally had brought in as many varieties of birds, trees and plants that would do well in this climate.

During the 1950s, we often had unusual birds flying over our yard morning and night, as regular as clockwork. In 1956, our next-door neighbor had hundreds of tropical birds in his aviary, and he felt the swooping birds had come "home to La Mirada"—they were offspring of some of McNally's birds. Imagine!

Our family quickly became friends with Bill Neff and with Jack and Anne George, who lived in the George House. Jack was the McNally Ranch manager and ran around the ranch in a jeep wearing his old sailor hat. (You can see him depicted on the mural in the La Mirada Post Office lobby, over the box section.) He enjoyed taking our boys for rides as much as the boys enjoyed being with him. They loved the wide-open spaces and the hiding places on the McNally Ranch.

After all the crops were picked, Jack George would tell the boys to come back at a certain time with buckets and then they could pick sweet corn, or tomatoes or whatever crop was left. Our family certainly appreciated all that fresh produce.

In 1953, shopping was done in neighboring Buena Park, Norwalk or Whittier. Valley View Farms with its cash-n-carry store was really welcomed when the dairy came to town in 1954.

TRIALS OF CONSTRUCTION

While we were building our house, developer Harold Shaw started building his houses on Alondra Boulevard (the Shaw I tract). Our water came from the well next to present-day Windermere Park. Shaw's trucks kept breaking the lines, so every evening our family would gather buckets, thermos jugs and any other containers we could and pull the coaster wagon over to Barnwall Street to the well to get water for that night and the next day. We were living in temporary quarters in a house at the other end of our block that our builder had not yet sold. We had only electricity, no gas, no telephones and, when the lines were broken, no water. We were a family of six.

T. Autry Mayes owned twenty-six acres, including our lot. We were not part of the subdivision. The Mayes family lived in the big La Pomelo home with its wrap-around porch next to the well and reservoir on Barnwall. His only daughter Tricia, for whom our street was named, was twelve years old at the time.

The Sphinx

Andrew McNally constructed the large house now known as the Neff Home in present-day Neff Park. Two large bronze sphinxes flanked Windermere Avenue leading in from Stage Road across from the railroad depot to this lovely turn-of-the-century home. When that part of town was being developed, the contractors moved the sphinx across the tracks into the old olive oil building. In 1958, they disappeared; they were so weighty, only heavy equipment could have handled them. Their disappearance caused much sadness to everyone wishing to preserve La Mirada's unique history.

A remnant of Windermere Avenue is still at Neff Park. As you drive into Neff Park and park near the house, the macadam (pavement) you see going nowhere is part of that road.

In 1953, when we came to La Mirada, that was the road from Stage Road in front of the railroad depot to the house. The sphinxes sat there majestically guarding the entrance to Andrew McNally's ranch.

Daphne Meiers and Marguerite Courson

Daphne and Marguerite George were born in the George House. Daphne lived in La Mirada longer than anyone, over seventy years Unfortunately, once she left she could never bring herself to go back and see the George House. Marguerite was the city clerk of Buena Park for over twenty-five years. Even after they were married, these girls spent some time living in the George House with their parents.

Jessie Benton

When we came to La Mirada in 1953, Jessie Benton, the bookkeeper for the McNally Ranch Company, still maintained her office in the olive oil pressing building across the tracks from the Santa Fe Depot. She drove her old 1941 Cadillac there every morning.

With the passing of Jessie Benton at the age of ninety-two, a bit of the serenity and fortitude that symbolized La Mirada over fifty years ago was gone. Before World War I, she lived in San Diego, California. In 1916, she came to La Mirada from Los Angeles to become the bookkeeper and secretary for the McNally Ranch Company and served in that capacity. For the next thirty-nine years, she never revealed the private business of the ranch. She was a confidante to Robert McGill, the resident manager of the McNally Ranch from 1901 to 1939, and for William Neff, grandson of Andrew McNally who managed the ranch from 1940 until it was subdivided in 1953. She had been hired through an employment agency for this position.

It was on Excelsior Drive that we first met her and listened raptly as she told of how beautiful the ranch had been and especially Lake Windermere, surrounded by trees and shrubs of almost every possible variety that would grow in this area. She believed that some of the unusually beautiful birds seen around the ranch are in La Mirada today and that they are descendants of the birds Andrew McNally imported from around the world some fifty years prior.

Santa Fe Railroad Depot/Post Office

If you go to the end of Biola Avenue and look to the right, this railroad station, which housed the La Mirada Post Office from 1893 to 1955, was nestled between four palm trees, which are still there and visible from Biola Avenue. Mail came to and from this community by way of the trains. Postmaster Lela Criswell hired me in January 1954 as the first clerk. I learned that our outgoing mail was put in a heavy canvas bag and closed with a heavy leather strap. We had to walk down the tracks and hang the mail sack with a special hook. If I didn't get it right, the bag would fall before the man on the train could grab it with his hook and pull it into the railroad mail car. Mail came to us in the same kind of bag, which they threw off to us.

Alice Palicz is hanging the mail bag so the Atchison Topeka and Santa Fe train can grab it when passing by at the La Mirada train depot on Stage Road, 1954. *Alice Palicz collection.*

1954—Dr. Sam Sutherland Came to Visit La Mirada

One day, unexpectedly, a train stopped at the depot and a group of men alighted. One stately gentleman introduced himself to Postmaster Lela Criswell as Dr. Sam Sutherland from the Bible Institute of Los Angeles (Biola). After looking around the depot for a minute, he commented, "You are going to have to get a bigger post office, because we will have one thousand students here in our college." With that, Dr. Sutherland and his contingency walked across Stage Road and down the way across the fields to inspect the property they were considering for a campus here in La Mirada, California, and I am sure they prayed over it.

Postmaster Extraordinaire: Lela Criswell

Lela was the kindest, hardest-working postmaster ever. There were several times when strangers, motorists, were stranded and came to the depot needing money. More than once I told Lela she wouldn't see that twenty dollars again, but she had faith in people. Invariably, they would come back, sometimes weeks later, to repay her.

La Mirada wasn't the only city with postal growing pains, but it was the only one growing at breakneck speeds without any mail delivery. From the start in the depot, we had to devise the best use of every inch of space possible.

Trying to satisfy 1,500 families in general delivery from a crowded storefront on Alondra, which was the only building available after we outgrew the depot, was a gigantic job. It could not have been done without Lela's husband, Vernon Criswell.

Loads of Mail—How We Handled It

By 1955, La Mirada received so much mail we had definitely outgrown the tossed bag system. The volume of mail was so heavy the outgoing mail could no longer be hung, and we were receiving too much for them to throw it off to us. The solution was for Santa Fe to put a big toolbox in front of the depot, and during the night, the train would stop and they would put all the mail in the toolbox. The box was approximately six feet long by four to five wide and about four feet deep.

Even after the post office moved to the store on Alondra, the amount of mail was a huge problem. All the young families in town were receiving packages from grandparents and ordering things for their new homes, and there was too little space to put any of it. At this time, it became necessary for Mr. Criswell and Mr. Palicz to take turns meeting the train at night, loading all the mail and parcels into their pickup trucks and taking the mail to the store on Alondra. Before Christmas and Christmas Eve night in 1955, they were delivering parcels as late as 11:00 p.m.

Serving 1,500 families in general delivery, postal inspectors from Los Angeles, who thought they knew everything about general delivery service, were breathing down our necks. We had to find what worked for us here in La Mirada, contrary to anything done in Los Angeles.

Child Disappears from the Nearby Town of Norwalk—Search Held on McNally Ranch

In 1953, Stella Darlene Nolan disappeared. It was feared she might have been taken here to the ranch and hidden among the trees and vegetation. Since my husband was a Los Angeles County sheriff reserve, he was asked to lead the search on the ranch. Don Criswell, who grew up here, knew the ranch like the back of his hand. The two of them searched in vain for the child. She was later found not far from her home under the approach to a bridge.

March 23, 1960: The City of Mirada Hills Was Incorporated

This momentous meeting was held at the Andrew McNally Intermediate School, which is now part of Biola University.

Since the new city had no money, they didn't think they needed a city treasurer, so they had not selected one. However, the city attorney advised them that night that they must have a treasurer. Councilwoman Estelle Troup was peeking out from behind the curtain and, seeing me in the front row, motioned for me to come up to the front. She explained the situation and said they would like me to fill that position.

Knowing this would involve lots of Tuesday night meetings, the council needed an answer right then. When she told me who their second choice might be, I immediately accepted this honorary unpaid position because the other person had lived in the area only a short time. I felt I was the more likely candidate.

Since the swearing in of a treasurer was not on the agenda, they forgot to call me up to be sworn in. The next day, City Clerk Anna J. Martin came to the post office and told Postmaster Criswell that she had to borrow me. So out in the parking lot of the post office, seated in Ann's convertible, I was sworn in as the first treasurer of the City of Mirada Hills, California, which later became the City of La Mirada, California.

I served that unpaid position for twenty-five years. All city business was done on my free time—in other words, lunchtime or annual leave from my duties at the post office.

On March 18, 1970, Estelle Troup had me signing one thousand checks a year without pay.

2

COUNCILMAN AND MAYOR—HIRAM'S AND LUCKY'S STORE MANAGER

1957–1986

By Lou Piltz

I arrived in La Mirada in October 1957 to begin my work as manager of the Hiram's Market in the new shopping Center. Hiram's was a six-unit independent grocery chain. This market was about fifty thousand square feet. All six Hiram's consisted of large stores compared with the conventional food markets of the day. The reason was that these stores were the forerunner of Big A, Price Club, Walmart, Sam's Club and Gemco. Product was stocked on the shelves by the whole case instead of a few rows of canned goods or boxes. The store layout included a food store, a liquor department, a camera department, a bakery, a snack bar, a jewelry section and a small non-foods department. Considering all of this, in my opinion and experience, it was the easiest store to manage.

One slight observation was that you also had to have good managers in all departments; in most cases, they came into their positions by promotions and performance. My Hiram's was one of the highest in volume and profits, which continued when Lucky Stores Incorporation purchased Hiram's in 1959. I stayed on as manager.

My thirteen years as manager of the store in La Mirada were the happiest and continued when I was assigned to open a new Lucky Store in Downey in 1972. I don't want to make it seem that I had the only good store because from the owners to the managers, we had the best and the happiest employees. Also, during my time in the food industry, I was robbed, chased shoplifters and got hit, and I tried to educate the young people just starting out in the work field. We had college graduates that wanted to start out as a manager or better. It took a little effort to convince them to start at the beginning and advance on their own merits. But one bit of advice was to the youngest element, to convince them to be after my job. That is one reason we had the best employees in our La Mirada market.

Hiram's also owned, Harris and Thomas, one of the largest wholesalers in Christmas trees and the most generous when it came to those in need at holiday time and during the entire year.

In late 1972, I was promoted to purchasing agent for the Lucky Stores southern division, which included Southern California, Nevada, Arizona and Texas. My next promotion was in 1974, when I was assigned as the maintenance manager in charge of all stores—Lucky's, Food Basket, Gemco and its Sporting Goods—in the same region. My job was to work with all the refrigeration, the roofing, the parking lot maintenance and general store conditions once a new store was opened. I went to Cypress College in Cypress, California, for refrigeration courses.

I retired in September 1986 from Lucky Stores Incorporation. To reiterate, I came to work in La Mirada in 1957. My wife and children lived in what became Long Beach. The area was annexed by Long Beach and included the area between Lakewood Boulevard and Palos Verdes Street and all the homes below Del Amo Boulevard. The other sections became the city of Lakewood.

While working in La Mirada, I had to travel through Dairy Valley; it was then two-lane asphalt roads, which were okay except when it rained hard or in the evening, during periods of fog, when I had to stop my automobile to make sure I stayed on the asphalt. There were other benefits to driving back and forth. I was able to relax and enjoy the dairy scenery. The cows and pastures and the quiet, and best of all were the new calves being born. I never complained.

After coming to La Mirada to work, before it was a city, I became involved with the Kiwanis Club, the chamber of commerce, the Shopping Center Association and political activity later on. Working and being involved, our family decided that we would move to La Mirada. La Mirada was incorporated in March 1960. In 1964, we did move to the La Mirada area. The great real estate firm Gomes for Homes sold me a house, after much discussion as to preference about locating in the city, in what was called "Mitchell's Island," a location almost in the exact center of La Mirada. The reason it was called Mitchells Island, was that Bob Mitchell, an attorney who lived in this area, worked hard to defeat the first incorporation election for the city, and when the city did win incorporation, Bob would have been on the new city council if his area had been included, which it was not at the beginning.

In 1970, I was appointed to the planning commission to replace a great guy, Dr. Sam Sutherland, the president of Biola University. Of interest I hope, my first city council meeting lasted until two o'clock the next morning. The hearing had to do with the annexation of the Foster Park area. This was a section of unincorporated LA County on the west side of La Mirada. It was a natural area for the city, but many residents of our city felt it would lower our standards and allow in the "bad" element. It was annexed, and the scare tactics did not come about. In fact, we, the city, through hard work and education of Foster Park residents have turned around the area and the skeptics. How could an area good or bad, up against the city, not have an effect on the whole city? Our present city manager, Tom Robinson, and I spent a lot of Saturdays sitting on Foster Park street corners greeting and meeting residents and giving out information and educating them about their city.

3

1927–1947

By Virginia Criswell Tressler

I was born on the Standard Oil lease located on Alondra and Lamont Streets and lived from age two months to twenty years within La Mirada's boundaries. My mother was Lela Criswell, postmaster of La Mirada. During these years, the La Mirada population consisted of the occupants of the six homes on the lease plus several "bunkhouses" for the single male workers, the McNally Home and homes for the workers on the ranch and a few private homes. There was a small country school, but by the time I went to school, the twenty or so children were bused to the K–8 grade school in Norwalk. The only businesses were the post office, the Standard Oil facility, and a facility that extracted olive oil. There were hundreds of olive trees in La Mirada and many acres of orange groves.

My mother's many friends often told her they thought it was an ideal place to have their children grow up in. Actually, it was lovely but very lonely for me. Except for the hours that the workmen were on the streets going to or leaving work, I could ride my bike on all the roads and sidewalks – something my friends who lived on dangerous city streets loved to do when they visited me.

My mother became postmaster of La Mirada in 1950. At that time, she served about fifty homes, but that changed rapidly by 1953 when the "building boom" began. Equipment was in short supply, and the population grew so rapidly that alphabetized shoeboxes took the place of

Vern and Lela Criswell at their house, which was actually on Standard Oil property, 1943. *Courtesy of Gail Pearce from the La Mirada City Archives.*

post office boxes. There was no mail delivery, so there were long lines waiting in general delivery lines.

One special memory of my mother, Lela, occurred Christmas Eve 1953. The last parcel post delivery did not reach the post office until long after closing time. Knowing that there were many homesick families that year in La Mirada, she organized friends and family and they home delivered every one of the Christmas packages that had arrived late. Many young families had a happier Christmas because of the kindness of these Santas.

4

MY MOM THE MAYOR

1954

By Barbara Troup Wilcox

There was many a day when I would think about my own mom, born in 1913, and her life in a world that was not particularly kind to women who wanted more than marriage and homemaking. Her journey would take her from teaching English in Buffalo, New York, to first lady mayor of La Mirada in 1965. My name is Barbara Troup Wilcox, and I am La Mirada's first lady mayor's daughter.

Mom was one of eight. There was no sexism in her household. She and her four sisters all graduated from college with various honors. Her father was a judge in Buffalo and raised his girls to view a world that was theirs to explore with no limits. Her mother was a dignified southern belle.

Soon, my father, Wes, found a job and we moved into our brand-new home in Shaw Tract 1 on Alondra Boulevard in La Mirada, California.

Those twelve years, from 1954 until 1965, when mom was mayor, cover the birth and early years of a new city. It was the perfect environment for my mother's amazing intellect, her pioneer spirit and her need to serve. I remember a very special moment when we first moved into La Mirada. Mom and Dad, sister Jane, brother Jack and I were all watching TV together in our new den, and out of the blue, Mom said, "My entire world is in this little room." It was lovely to remember, as we were about to share our mom with so many.

Over the years, I have been asked many times, "What was it like to have your mom be the mayor?" She was of course first and foremost "Mom."

The many hours on the phone or off to meetings dealing with the newspaper and city issues took her away from us but also introduced us to a world of wonderful people who joined forces to create the City of La Mirada.

Our mother was beyond special, and I cannot put into words the dynamics of her presence. She raised a family in the fifties and sixties while teaching Latin and journalism full time at Excelsior High School. She wrote a weekly column, Small Print, for the *La Mirada Lamplighter* and became a member of the first city council of La Mirada. All the while I thought this was normal. Now looking back on my own experiences as a working mother, I am completely in awe of her accomplishments. To document mom's journey is a book in itself. There were phone calls, thousands of phone calls at the house, about city business or newspaper issues.

I think it was Abraham Lincoln who said, "All that I am or hope to be I owe to my mother." I was blessed with two wonderful parents, but to have such a special lady as a role model for what a woman could do or become was a true gift. I see many qualities of my mom in my daughter Kate, a mom and English teacher herself now, and in my nieces and granddaughters. To Mom and to all of the women who forged the way for girls everywhere to achieve their dreams, I am humbly grateful.

She wanted to be buried at Olive Lawn Cemetery so she could "look over her city." We honored her request.

5

HOW JEROME O. OXMAN STARTED HIS MILITARY SURPLUS STORE

By Jerome O. Oxman (1915–2013)

In 1960, Miriam, my wife, and I rented a spot at 1609 East Slauson in Los Angeles. I wasn't too pleased with it at all. We were only there for about nine months. It was a little building—we did our best though. We fixed it up and organized it. We fixed up the washroom and made it beautiful.

It was located just off the main street. I put up signs and tried to promote it to the public. It didn't matter how nice we made it, people were just not coming. I had a lot of equipment that I had purchased from Douglas Aircraft. We filled up the store and the side yard too.

Finally, it got too hairy, and I decided that I was going to move. I had to have a place for all the equipment. We had just bought a home in La Mirada, and a friend had a big garage behind their house for rent. It was in Buena Park near Beach Boulevard and Ninth or Tenth Street. I started to get all of the equipment out of the yard on Slauson. While I was loading a truck to move the equipment, two boys came by and wanted to know if I needed some help. I told them that I sure did. They loaded everything on the truck for me, and they were fast too. I got out of there in no time. I think I paid them ten dollars each, and they were thrilled to death. I fixed up the garage in our new house on Manacita Drive like a shipping office. I advertised in the *Lamplighter* and the *Pennysaver* and other papers and started a mail-order business. I did a pretty good mail-order business right from the garage. I sold a lot of aircraft equipment, instruments, hydraulics, motors, fittings, you name it—I sold it. It was just fantastic—whatever I bought, I was able to sell.

I still remember the post office box; it was no. 55, in La Mirada, California. I used it quite a number of years. Every day I had packages going out. It worked out just great. But in one case, I bought some airplane toilet seats. They were a white elephant. I just could not get rid of them, so I buried them behind the garage that I was renting in Buena Park (and they are probably still there).

Mr. Arnoff was in charge of the property on Rosecrans and Valley View. The Big A was on the south side. The warehouse for Big A and 9 garages were on the north side of the lot, and I wanted to rent one of the garages. I spoke with the manager of the Big A to see if it was possible to rent one of the garages. He told me he didn't see why not. He said that I would just have to see Mr. Arnoff. I tried for days, but I could never get a hold of him. He was never in the store, and he didn't answer the phone, and he would not return my messages. Somehow I was able to obtain his home address. The only way that I could see him was to go over to his home. I went at seven o'clock one morning because I wanted that little garage so bad. I got in the car and drove to Beverly Hills. He had a mansion there. It was seven o'clock in the morning, and I rang the doorbell. A maid came to the door. She said, "Yes, what is it?" I said, "I would like to speak with Mr. Arnoff." She asked me if I had an appointment, and I said no and that I hadn't been able to get in touch with him. I said that it was important and that I would like to talk with him. She said that it was too early and Mr. Arnoff was not ready to see anyone. I asked her to just tell him that I was there. She said that she would tell him and see what he wanted to do. I guess she went to him and told him how adamant I was, and he said, "OK." I went in, and he was in a robe and on the phone. He hung up the phone and said to me, "What the heck are you doing here so early in the morning?" I told him that I wanted to rent a portion of his building. He said, "You do?" He asked me if my business would interfere with his business. I told him, "Not at all." I told him that I had seen one of his garages and that I would like to use them for mail order. (I fibbed a little bit on that one because I wanted to start a retail store.) He said, "OK" and then said, "Anyone that had the gall to arrive at my house at seven in the morning deserves to get what they wanted," and then he said, "The rent will be one hundred dollars per month, and you can have the garage."

The next day, I talked to the manager of Big A. He told me that Mr. Arnoff had told him all about me and that I had the guts to come and talk to him at his home.

I put an ad in the paper that said "Something New Is Coming to La Mirada." Miriam did the drawings for the ads. The drawings were so vivid and good that people started calling like crazy. People started asking what was going on, and I gave them the address. They came by, and they asked, "What is new that is coming in here?" I told them that I would let them know when I was ready. I bought some tables from Douglas on a bid. There were long and real heavy. I got a truck and brought all those tables in and lined up all the tables and started putting equipment on them. I borrowed a cash register from the Big A because I didn't have one. The manager was real nice about it. We loaded up all the tables with everything we had. People started coming. I was open from ten o'clock to seven o'clock, three days a week. The rest of the time was for mail order. People started asking me to stay open so that they could come in on Saturday. I told them maybe someday I would do that.

I was buying stuff from Douglas on bid. I put in a lot of equipment, everything that I could get a hold of. I even went out and scouted some of the local companies. One was making doors, and they had overages that they would sell to me for a couple bucks each. I sold them for ten or twelve dollars each.

People came in just like crazy, and they had such a good time in the store, it was phenomenal. Miriam was very instrumental in my success. She did all the drawings. She did all of the advertising and printing. Nobody knows just how much she did.

Around 1965, we started negotiating with the new property owners, Jenkelson in San Francisco, for the purchase of the big building next to our garages. We were successful in purchasing the north end of the lot. It included the nine garages, one large warehouse building with offices on the second floor, a large storage yard and a little tiny house. One night, Miriam and I started to move our operation out of the garages to the big building. We had to move the tables and all the merchandise. As we brought the tables in, we would bring the merchandise in. How we did it…I don't know. We worked all night long, and believe it or not, we did it! Miriam was phenomenal. She would carry things that no man could carry, and that is where we are today.

Back then, the *Pennysaver* was upstairs, and there was a real estate company run by Vita Garret in the bottom offices. They all eventually moved out. I had the old sign torn down and had a new sign made and put it on the pole. The sign is still there today. The whole upstairs was available, so we stored equipment up there. I had a lot of wheels, small plastic wheels. I bought them for practically nothing, and we sold them like wildfire. People would come in and they would buy twenty or twenty-five of them. They bought them all, and they were all stored upstairs. I bought drills along the way.

Every time they were on sale, I would buy them by the hundreds. I kept winning bids. I paid enough to outbid all the other people. There would be twenty or twenty-five stores bidding against me, and I won every single one of them. I had enough drill bits to last a lifetime. Even today, we are still selling drill bits from the early days.

We were open seven days a week, but we closed about five or six o'clock on Sundays. We were open to nine o'clock on the weekdays. Miriam would bring me lunch and dinner to the store. She would come with our three little children, Murray, Ricky and Jason. We had a good time. I enjoyed what I was doing, and I made money at it. We were very happy.

I was always involved with the city of La Mirada. I was a board member of the La Mirada Meals on Wheels. I donated a lot of time and money to the organization, fifty dollars every month for a number of years. I have been a member of the La Mirada Chamber of Commerce since we moved into La Mirada, and I am still a member in good standing. I was a chamber president two or three times. The strange part is, our business is located in Santa Fe Springs, not La Mirada, but we felt a strong connection to La Mirada. I was also a member of the Santa Fe Springs Chamber of Commerce and have been since 1961.

I was on the La Mirada Hospital Board of Trustees. I was an active member, and we had meetings once a month. For several years, I awarded one hundred dollars per month to the most amiable nurse, chosen by her peers at the La Mirada Hospital. It was just my way for trying to enhance the hospital and make the people that worked there a little cognizant of what was going on.

I was a one-year member of La Mirada Kiwanis Club. I also gave speeches all around the community. I was invited to speak in La Mirada, Buena Park and Fullerton. Charitable organizations called me and asked me to attend many breakfast meetings. I would give a good half-hour speech about my activities. They were crazy about me, and I would usually get a coffee mug for my appearances. They were really appreciative when I came.

I am a fifty-year sponsor of La Mirada Little League Baseball. In 2003, we sponsored a team that went all the way and became champions of the Little League Juniors Division. I received a real nice trophy, and Miriam and I were invited to dinner because they won the championship that year. They thought so much of me that they asked me if I would be willing to go to Dodger Stadium to be honored. I said, "Of course." They brought us out onto the playing field and took pictures of us before the baseball game. That was in 2005. My picture and name were up on the big screen at the stadium. They gave us a nice round of applause. It was very satisfying to be recognized and honored that way.

In 1985, I was a sponsor for the Miss La Mirada Contest, under the care of Fran Mock. I judged four different pageants.

In 1961, I started a rifle drill team with the La Mirada Cub Scouts. We practiced at La Pluma School. There were eleven kids, including two of my sons, Murray and Ricky, and they were all excited. I ordered eleven parade rifles. They were $12.89 each. They were beautiful little rifles. They looked a lot like the 30 aught 6 that was used in the army. They were all-wood rifles. They were drill rifles. The boys were just thrilled with them. We started practicing, and they paid close attention. They listened and soaked in everything I taught them about handling a rifle. I went through the whole manual for their experience, and they watched me and copied me for each activity. They did quite well. There was a manual for "right shoulder" and a manual for the "left shoulder." There was a manual for "present arms" and a manual for "rest" (how to put the rifle down and just hold onto it). I showed them how to stack the rifles. They were so excited that they couldn't wait for the class. We had class each day after school. I left my business and went over to the school, which was about a mile and a half from my store. They did so well that one of the companies in La Mirada asked me if I would be in a parade that they were sponsoring. I told them that we would be in the parade. On a Saturday, we were in that parade, and I had a shirt that was all sparkles and silver. The kids were all dressed in the same type of shirt. They looked terrific. We paraded down La Mirada Boulevard. They did extremely well, and we had lots of applause as we went by. The kids were just thrilled. One day the head of the Scouts USA directed me to stop the drill team classes because it was too military. They told me that they didn't want the children to learn how to handle a rifle. We had to stop, but the boys kept their rifles. They came into the store and told me they were all together and still practicing.

Today, in 2013, we are still going strong. We are still in the exact same location and we just remodeled the store. The entrance used to be on the parking lot side of the building. Now our entrance faces Rosecrans Avenue. We also made changes to the inside of the store. We added a two-thousand-square-foot museum, and it is the entrance to the store. All of my personal collection is on display for all to see, free of charge. We have hundreds of pieces of military memorabilia on display. We have a B-17 Bomber Cockpit, a B-29 Bomber radial engine, ejection seats, a Norden Bomb Sight, a Bull-Pup "air to ground missile," World War I and II uniforms and helmets, original newspapers from Pearl Harbor, World War II extras and the Space Race, plus German bayonets and medals and the list goes on and on. I have been collecting for fifty years. I would buy stuff, and my family would say, "What are you buying that for?" I would always answer them, "Someday I will have my own museum."

And thanks to my family and especially Miriam and our two boys, Murray and Jason, who have made Oxman's Surplus their careers. We have a most magnificent museum and a snack bar called the Mess Tent Café. It is their vision and fortitude that has brought us into the twenty-first century while respecting the history of our country and our little business here in La Mirada bordering on Santa Fe Springs, California.

6

THE WAYNE GRISHAM LEGACY

1956–2012

In 1956, a young entrepreneur named Wayne Grisham opened one of the first real estate offices in a growing new city called La Mirada. What started as a small, one-man office blossomed into a thriving business and launched Wayne into leadership positions and elected offices from La Mirada to Sacramento to Washington D.C and Kenya, Africa. As a public servant over the next four decades, Wayne Grisham came to be a household name for most of the residents of La Mirada.

It's quite common for the Grisham family to find La Mirada homeowners who tell stories of Wayne going above and beyond to help them to purchase their home. He took pride in his job and in helping people. His ever-present smile and positive attitude were a comfort to his clients and his constituents. Wayne was a man who loved serving his community.

A decorated World War II pilot, Wayne's services in the military helped shape his beliefs in a strong America. As a fighter pilot, he was shot down over Germany and became a prisoner of war. Miraculously surviving the crash, he later told his young bride, Millie, that "God is my copilot!" For his meritorious service, he received the Purple Heart and Air Medal.

A star athlete at Long Beach Jordan High School, Wayne went on to graduate from Whittier College with a degree in economics. Wayne taught fifth and sixth grades before deciding to get into real estate. With his background in economics and an interest in government, Grisham's early career included involvement in the California Jaycees, the board of realtors and chambers of commerce. A strong business orientation combined with his efforts in the community made Grisham a popular choice for president of these organizations, and he often served in leadership roles.

One of the more popular city leaders of La Mirada, Wayne Grisham, in 1965. *Courtesy of Gail Pearce from the La Mirada City Archives.*

Wayne moved his family to La Mirada in 1966 with his wife, Millie, and children, Cathy, Randy and Kellie. Grisham's political life started in 1970 when he was elected to the La Mirada City Council. He served two terms as mayor (1973–74, 1977–78) and enjoyed his role immensely. Some of the milestones to occur during his tenure were the development of the La Mirada Civic Theater, which became the La Mirada Theater for the Performing Arts, and the building of the stadium in La Mirada High School.

La Mirada Lamplighter's Richard "Dick" Hurley, senior editor from 1955 to 1980, pictured here in 1963. *Courtesy of Gail Pearce from the La Mirada City Archives.*

In 1978, he was asked by civic leaders to run for U.S. Congress. He was elected handily and was reelected in 1980 to serve a second term in the U.S. House of Representatives, representing the 33rd district of California. Wayne served proudly under President Jimmy Carter and President Ronald Reagan.

Millie recalls that Wayne spent many evenings in their home with fellow La Mirada realtor Wayne Young and *La Mirada Lamplighter* editor Dick Hurley, discussing politics and other related things going on in La Mirada. When Wayne was elected to Congress as a Republican, Dick Hurley told him he might now have to report things not as a friend of Wayne's but as a critic, since Dick was a liberal. Wayne much preferred the nonpartisan way of government that he enjoyed while on the La Mirada City Council. He brought that sense of community with him to Washington, D.C., and was known for reaching across the aisle. His priority was to serve the people of his district, not the people of his party.

A self-described "do-gooder," he once told the *LA Times*, "I think of myself as an average guy, and I think it was the average guy who elected me."

Fellow congressman David Drier had this to say, "Wayne was the model of civility." Although they were forced to run against each other because of redistricting, Grisham was "a friend and colleague...he was a true gentleman. We remained friends throughout the campaign and after."

In 1983, President Reagan appointed Grisham the Peace Corps director of Kenya, Africa. Wayne had the pleasure of overseeing three hundred volunteers, and he and Millie visited many of them serving in remote parts of Kenya.

In 1984, Wayne was elected to the California State Assembly, where he represented La Mirada and served for four years. He retired from politics in 1988. He would often joke, "I'm retired due to illness....The people are sick of me!" Wayne continued to be active in the real estate industry for another decade, and then he retired completely and headed for the golf course.

Wayne wasn't the only Grisham to be active in La Mirada. It seems a dedication to community service, volunteerism and accepting leadership roles (and being a realtor) run in the Grisham family.

Millie was a tremendous advocate for the city as well. She was as an active volunteer and member of the Republican Women, the La Mirada Methodist Church, the PTA, and for many years, she and Myllie Taylor ran the "Angel Tree" program in the La Mirada Mall. In Washington, D.C., Millie served as president of the California Congressional Wives. However, the job she loved the most was raising her children.

Wayne and Millie instilled a strong sense of community and service in their children. A love of God, a love of country and a love of family were traits that the Grishams imparted. All three Grisham children were raised in La Mirada. They each married, bought their own homes and settled in La Mirada. With such a devotion to their hometown, all three Grisham children have been active in the community, much like their father, and as a result they all have been recognized for their efforts and their leadership abilities.

Wayne and Millie were married for sixty-six years until his passing in January 2011 at the age of eighty-eight. He had the pleasure of watching his children and grandchildren grow up in the city that he had such affection for. Together, they taught their family to love our city and to volunteer and be involved.

Wayne's dedication to his city was not forgotten. In early 2012, the La Mirada City Council, together with our local congresswoman, Linda Sanchez, proposed legislation to the House of Representatives to designate the U.S. Post Office in La Mirada as the "Wayne Grisham Post Office." The measure was passed overwhelmingly by Congress.

Congresswoman Sanchez offered, "Wayne Grisham was a man of principle and great personal integrity.…Every public servant should show the same dedication as Wayne showed for our local community."

7

NOTICE FROM THE AREA'S FIRST TELEGRAM

The Lemon Grove Boyhood of Wallace Neff

Edwin Wallace Neff, destined to become one of Southern California's premier architects, was born on January 28, 1895, in a new home in a new settlement on a broad plain seventeen miles southeast of Los Angeles, California. "A healthy eight pound son," Neff's parents, Ed and Nannie, wired to the baby's grandparents in Altadena, California, and Chicago, Illinois. It was the first telegram with a La Mirada, California dateline.

Only weeks before, Ed, Nannie and their one-year-old son, Andrew Neff, arrived at La Mirada to set up a household and await buyers for the land their family controlled. The number of inhabitants on the outpost could not have been over fifty. Sheep had the land to themselves for decades after Abel Stearns's Rancho Los Coyotes was racked by flood and drought and lost to bankruptcy. Then in 1888, Nannie's father, Andrew McNally, co-founder of Rand, McNally and Company, the mapmakers, purchased the land. Shrewdly, Andrew McNally had waited until the land boom collapsed and the price of the remote flat land reached rock bottom.

The Neff Home sat at the center of Windermere Ranch, a 2,600-acre compound within McNally's speculative 1,500-acre country gentlemen's estates. Ed and Nannie could peer from the baby's room in their large new La Mirada home.

8

LA MIRADA-BORN JENNIE FINCH

The Softball Diva

Jennie attended La Mirada High School and has dominated so completely the sport of softball she took the two words *athletes* and *charisma* to a new level.

Jennie Finch is arguably the most recognizable softball player in the world. She went 2-0 for the U.S. softball team in 2004, helping it win the gold medal in Athens.

Her number, 27, was retired in 2003 by the University of Arizona, where she was a three-time All-American pitcher and a first baseman. She also earned the Honda Award as the nation's best softball player in 2001, when the Wildcats won the national title, and in 2002.

Finch set an CAA record with 60 consecutive pitching wins over three seasons. She earned 109 total victories, 12th most at the time, including 32 wins (and no losses) in her junior season to set another NCAA record. She struck out 1,028 along the way.

"It's special what she's done here," Mike Candrea, coach of Arizona and the U.S. team, said of Finch's college days. "And it's special for the game of softball."

Finch was born in La Mirada, California, and began playing softball at five. Her father, Doug, was her first pitching coach. He also invented the Finch Windmill, an arm conditioning device that Jennie began using at ten.

At La Mirada High School, she pitched six perfect games and thirteen no-hitters. Part of Finch's allure is her marketability. She was named one of *People's* most beautiful people in 2004, was on the cover of *Sports Illustrated*

La Mirada celebrity Jennie Finch. She played softball at La Mirada High School, and her pitching for Team USA won gold medals at the 2004 and 2008 Summer Olympics. *From the* New York Times.

in 2005 and has appeared on a number of television shows, including *This Week in Baseball* and *Pros vs. Joes*.

Jennie, the "Underhand Pitching Hurler," has the distinction of striking out Albert Pujols.

9

NEW INVESTMENT

The La Mirada Library Open Book Proposal

After seven years of planning and renovating, the official dedication occurred with a soft opening on November 21, 2016.

The library has been closed since December 31, 2015, due to renovations within fourth district Los Angeles County supervisor Don Knabe's Operation Libraries project. The renovations include designated areas for children, teens and adults, study and conference rooms and a new bookstore for the Friends of the La Mirada Library group.

"I think that there's a lot more open space and a lot more flexible space so they'll be able to use it differently than traditional libraries," said Skye Patrick, Los Angeles County library director. "I think they're really going to like the fact that we now have a designated children's area, designated teen area and designated adult area."

To start off the dedication ceremony, Patrick welcomed local community members and officials and talked about the importance of staying persistent to complete a project. Sonora High School senior Emma Reynosa Avila spoke on how the library has become a place for the community rather than simply a place that holds books.

A Dream

"The reopening will bring back people to the library and even more people because there's going to be so many new things that people are going to want to be attracted to, and so the more people in the library is good and I want to help attract them," Avila said.

With the new additions, Knabe described the completion of this project as a dream. Patrick also mentioned the library now includes twelve new adult computers and seven new children's computers and the library book collection has gone up to eighty-five thousand.

"I think that this is one of those communities that already love their library, so anything that we do will just serve as an enhancement," Patrick said.

Following this, the mayor of La Mirada, Steve De Ruse, shared about his gladness on the library reopening and appreciation of the hard work that went into the project.

"I hope it will spur more people to come down here, take advantage of the resources. It's an educational tool, it is kind of the hub of the city and it always has been. There are a lot of things here for all ages and I just hope the community really takes advantage of it because it is something that is going to last for quite a while," De Ruse said.

Hal Malkin, president of Friends of the La Mirada Library, also spoke on the lasting importance of the library. Malkin encouraged the community to support the library as it remains a heritage of the past and a promise of the future. The renovations include a space for the Friends of the Library to have a bookstore, which members showed excitement for, including book sale runner Lynn Allen.

La Mirada Library was converted into a modern state-of-the-art facility, 2016. *From the* Biola University Chimes.

"I'm really excited, I can't wait," Allen said. "Hopefully we will bring in, let's say, a couple hundred dollars a week, hopefully more than that. That would amount to quite a bit of money for the library."

While people remain excited about the current state of renovations, projects remain, such as putting in the ceiling in the teen workroom, adding more fixtures, painting and adding smart boards in the study rooms, with an official opening in the spring, according to Patrick. However, the current renovations already stun people, including library worker Laura Moran.

"Oh my gosh, it's absolutely amazing," Moran said. "Everything is brand new and everything, it's just, I don't really have words. It's really nice, I'm really happy that everything turned out amazing."

Addendum

LA MIRADA'S CITY SEAL

The Dove

The Dove has seemingly inexhaustible sources of symbolic flavor throughout most histories, cultures and myth.

Doves are commonly considered a symbol of motherhood because of their unique ability to produce their own milk. Another confirmation about maternal attributes, as well as self-sacrifice for the sake of their offspring, is that they cease foraging for food just before their babies are born. This temporary starvation ensures a purer milk formulation for their offspring.

Historically, dove symbolism is associated with several mother figures:

- The Mother Mary in Christian legend (care, devotion, purity and peace)
- Ishtar in Assyrian culture (promise of hope and salvation)
- Aphrodite and Venus (viewing the soul or a sense of higher love)
- The softly lulling coos of the dove are testimony to a divinely calming presence among us. In fact, their soft vocalizations and docile appearance enhances their interpretation as celestial messengers—or the symbolic link between earth and air. The dove is a symbol of the soul's release from its earth-bound duty.

- On earth, they are intimately aware of their environment and demonstrate a highly developed sense of presence. As creatures of both the earth and the air, doves serve as liaisons between intuitive thought and common reality. This ability to move between two worlds (sky and earth), bird totems are uniquely posed to funnel higher knowledge down to our human conscious awareness. They link intangible knowing (thought, dreams, intuition) with physical practicality (hearth, home, security). Doves represent the balance between thought (air) and matter (earth).
- Bridging this link between the higher mind and the more practical level in which we live makes the dove a perfect guide for dream interpretation as well. Bird totems offer inspiration combined with a grounding element to make new ideas implementable.

The dove represents peace of the deepest kind. It soothes and quiets our worried or troubled thoughts, enabling us to find renewal in the silence of the mind. The dove's singing is most prevalent when the veils between the physical and spiritual worlds are thought to be at their thinnest—first thing in the morning and last thing at night—again representing a link between two divergent domains.

Doves teach us that, regardless of external circumstances, peace is always a touch a way—within us—and always available. It is said that if a dove flies into your life, you are being asked to go within and release your emotional disharmony. The dove helps us to rid the trauma stored deep within our cellular memory. Doves carry the energy of promise. When inner conflicts are banished from our thoughts, words and feelings, goodness awaits.

The dove's roles as spirit messenger, maternal symbol and liaison impart an inner peace that helps us to go about our lives calmly and with purpose.

AFTERWORD

Raymond Fernandez

For the last thirteen years, I have been driving through La Mirada. I sensed that the city was rich with history and that in itself, was something quite proud to be a part of. Many times I wondered and wished that somehow the past could be unlocked, from a historical perspective. While Glen Cantrell and I had developed a friendship, and knowing that he was an accomplished author, I posed this question to him, "Glen, how about a book about La Mirada's history as well as the residents, as many as we can find; who would want to do this and write about their own experiences within this fine community? Their own likings and thoughts about their surroundings?" This was back in October 2010. Glen stated, "You know, Raymond, now you got me thinking." He and I launched our idea in May 2011, and it was later that year in Neff Park where we started formulating a game plan. The idea had been born in my mind from so many of the historical and present-day pictures that Glen had been posting on Facebook. I quickly realized that we both have a love and passion for the great city of La Mirada, the "Courtesy Capitol of the World."

I'd like to express gratitude to the great City of La Mirada and all the love we have for it. Also, I would like to include my father, George and Eva Sanchez, my grandparents Patty Verdugo and Sylvia Hernandez, my aunts, as well as George Sanchez and Danny Sanchez, both my uncles. Also a big shoutout to La Mirada High School Class of 1993—We go together.

Thank you, God, for putting these people in my life, and seeing this book through to its fruition.

GLEN CANTRELL

I remember growing up in an exceptionally friendly and easy-on-the-eye municipality. I recall it being a very tidy city tucked away from the skyscraping bustling avenues and freeways, along with a clean spacious home to live in a pleasant neighborhood with certainly pleasant people. There was a kind of charm about this city and a feeling of unfailing safeness wherever you were, night or day.

I call to mind special hangouts and hideouts in this town and the childhood friends I made. There was the one usual grouch on my particular cul-de-sac and the one bully, but not anyone I ever had considerable trouble keeping clear of, or from, among a group of buddies.

In a very short walking distance from my parents' home, there was a park called Gardenhill. Olives were everywhere on the grass that fell from the infinite amount of olive trees that dotted the fertile recreational area. As Terry Henne, a fine member of the community, coined, "There were purple sidewalks," from the crushed olive juices, transferred from the bottom of all our shoes and on to the walkways.

This community I was raised in is in Los Angeles County and borders Orange County, California, to the south and the east and the city of Whittier to the north. The town is La Mirada, and the state is California, Southern California to be exact.

Six cherished decades in this ideal city, the nation's first completely planned city: La Mirada, which in the Spanish vernacular means "the mirror," or, as some might argue, "the view." It was in 1979 when I moved from La Mirada to Laguna Hills, California. I've been trying to move back to the city where I grew up ever since and am still striving to—to this very day.

BIBLIOGRAPHY

Aiello, Tony. "AdviceRadio.com Cor Van Dam Interview 2005." Transcribed by Glen Cantrell. In Cantrell, Fernandez and Aiello, *Reflections from McNally's Mirror*, 121–30.

———. "AdviceRadio.com Jerome O. Oxman Interview, September 2, 2003." Transcribed by Glen Cantrell. In Cantrell, Fernandez and Aiello, *Reflections from McNally's Mirror*, 113–20.

Camp, C.W. "Bob." "City of La Mirada Historical Committee Press Releases 1966." In Cantrell, Fernandez and Aiello, *Reflections from McNally's Mirror*, 49–56.

———. "The George Home and Windermere Ranch." In Cantrell, Fernandez and Aiello, *Reflections from McNally's Mirror*, 46.

———. "La Mirada Was a Movie Location." In Cantrell, Fernandez and Aiello, *Reflections from McNally's Mirror*, 52.

———. "Neff Park Subdivions 1953–1960 La Mirada Tracts of Homes." In Cantrell, Fernandez and Aiello, *Reflections from McNally's Mirror*, 41.

———. "'The Olive and Its Oil,' They Started La Mirada 'Ended in an Earthquake.'" In Cantrell, Fernandez and Aiello, *Reflections from McNally's Mirror*, 111.

———. "The Peeblers: Byron and Ethel Peebler of Olive Lawn Cemetery." In Cantrell, Fernandez and Aiello, *Reflections from McNally's Mirror*, 104–10.

———. "Robert McGill also Known as R.C. McGill and the 'Czar of La Mirada.'" In *La Mirada: From Rancho to City*, 42–44. Fullerton, CA: Sultana Press, 1970.

———. "Trinidad Villegas." In Cantrell, Fernandez and Aiello, *Reflections from McNally's Mirror*, 53.

Campbell, Kellie Grisham, and Millie Grisham. "The Wayne Grisham Legacy 1956–2012." In Cantrell, Fernandez and Aiello, *Reflections from McNally's Mirror*, 218–22.

Cantrell, Glen, Raymond Fernandez and Tony Aiello, eds. *Reflections from McNally's Mirror*. Bloomington, IN: Xlibris Corporation, 2013.

Carden, Allen. "Changing and Concerning Times from Preincorporation, During Incorporation and Postincorporation, along with the 1960s, the 1970s and the 1980s up to 1985." In *The City of La Mirada: A Silver Anniversary History, 1960–1985*. La Mirada, CA: La Mirada City Council, 1986.

———. "Population, Parks and Recreation, Cultural Activities, Commercial Development, Education and Annexations to the City of La Mirada" In *The City of La Mirada: A Silver Anniversary History, 1960–1985*. La Mirada, CA: La Mirada City Council, 1986.

Desert Sun. "Foreign Dairy Farmers Found Home in State—Plenty of Good Level Land for New Operations." September 25, 1978. https://cdnc.ucr.edu.

Harris, Robert. "La Pomelo Ranch: A Showplace Retreat in Old La Mirada." In Cantrell, Fernandez and Aiello, *Reflections from McNally's Mirror*, 57–59.

Hoppert, Melissa. "Athlete Bio: Jennie Finch." *New York Times*, August 3, 2008. www.nytimes.com.

Kanner, Diane. "Notice from the Area's First Telegram." *Southern California Quarterly*, 80 no. 4 (Winter 1998): 435–60.

Los Angeles Herald. "Three Most Charming Places of this Southern Land." June 8, 1902.

McNally, Andrew. "Andrew McNally Tells How He Became a Ranchman in Southern California." *Los Angeles Herald*, February 14, 1904. https://cdnc.ucr.edu.

Minneapolis (MN) Journal. "Edgebrook Ranch—Most Famous Places in Southern California." January 28, 1905. https://chroniclingamerica.loc.gov.

Mitchell, Rebecca. "New Investment: The La Mirada Library Open Book Proposal from Library Becomes an Open Book—La Mirada Library Opens with Major Changes Complete." *Chimes*, 2016. https://chimesnewspaper.com.

Mystic Familiar. "Animal Totems: Dove." www.mysticfamiliar.com/library/shamanism/animal_totems.htm#Dove.

Oxman, Jerome O., Jason, Murray and Miriam Oxman. "A Dedication Remembrance: The Oxman Family of Oxman's Surplus Mr. O's Stories." In Cantrell, Fernandez and Aiello, *Reflections from McNally's Mirror*, 9–14.

Pacific Rural Press. "Boom in Olive Planting." March 7, 1896. https://cdnc.ucr.edu.

———. "Crushing Olives Olive Pressing Underway La Mirada, Calif." February 15, 1902. https://cdnc.ucr.edu.

———. "Manure Spreader Does Better Work, Why Dump Manure in Piles—Engine Would Save Horses." November 6, 1920. https://cdnc.ucr.edu.

———. "A Remembrance of Andrew McNally—The Farm in Summer." August 4, 1900. https://cdnc.ucr.edu.

———. "Scutellista Saves Orchardist." January 7, 1905. https://cdnc.ucr.edu.

Palicz, Alice. "Anna J. Martin 'La Mirada's First City Clerk' '1960, 2012.'" In Cantrell, Fernandez and Aiello, *Reflections from McNally's Mirror*, 188–216.

———. "La Mirada Memories 1953 Moving Onwards Through Time 1953." In Cantrell, Fernandez and Aiello, *Reflections from McNally's Mirror*.

Piltz, Lou. "La Mirada Councilman and Mayor—Hiram's and Lucky's Store." In Cantrell, Fernandez and Aiello, *Reflections from McNally's Mirror*, 224–36.

Remley, Don. "The Beginnings at the Turn of the Century: A History of La Mirada, California. Andrew McNally's Colony Plan and the Windermere Ranch 1890, 1905." *Lamplighter*, December 4, 1967.

Republican Journal (Belfast, ME). "The Windermere Ranch." March 1, 1900. https://chroniclingamerica.loc.gov.

San Bernardino (CA) Sun. "La Mirada, CA Interview with Freda Terenzio, a La Mirada Citizen—Dial-A-Ride May Solve Bus Problems." October 1, 1973. https://cdnc.ucr.edu.

San Francisco Call. "Millionaire McNally, the Chicago Publisher, After a Rest on His Olive and Lemon Ranch." April 3, 1896. https://cdnc.ucr.edu.

Shamanic Journey. "Shamanism Is Not a Belief System." http://www.shamanicjourney.com.

Smithson, Jess. *The Folks at Valley View Farms Present a Brief History of La Mirada*. La Mirada, CA: self-published, 1954.

Tokach, Marilyn. "The Dove." Pure Spirit Animal Communications & Behavior Solutions, http://www.pure-spirit.com/602-dove-symbolism.

Tressler, Virginia Criswell. "1927–1947." In Cantrell, Fernandez and Aiello, *Reflections from McNally's Mirror*, 176–78.

What's-Your-Sign. "Animal Totems." http://www.whats-your-sign.com/animal-totems.html.

Wilcox, Barbara Troup. "My Mom the Mayor." In Cantrell, Fernandez and Aiello, *Reflections from McNally's Mirror*, 183–97.

ABOUT THE AUTHORS

A lover of all history worldwide, GLEN CANTRELL once aspired to be a history teacher for grades seven and eight. After Glen spent his first twenty-one years in the city of La Mirada, California, he moved out to Page, Arizona, in 1982. Glen learned how to co-pilot an inland lake fifty-foot vessel at Lake Powell National Recreation Area in Arizona, but mainly in the state of Utah. Page, Arizona, is close to the border of those two states. He then became a canyon tour guide on the lake. He drove a Uniflite Tour boat, which accommodated up to fifty-five passengers, and would take them on an eight-hour exploration, the high point being Rainbow Bridge National Monument, one of the largest natural arches in the United States. Beginning in the 1990s, Glen delivered home health care in Los Angeles and Orange County, California. At the peak of the 1990s, his vocation was in the security field, and during graveyard shifts, he began to write. Glen has completed two published fiction novels, one being a science fiction chronicle. Today, he is a security professional and a novelist.

RAYMOND FERNANDEZ moved to La Mirada in November 1981 during the year of the El Niño Rains. He lived in La Mirada from 1981 to 1996 and then came back to La Mirada from 2016 to the present time. He currently sits on the La Mirada Historical Preservation Council

Committee. He has been in the insurance industry for the last twenty-seven years and was born in 1975. Raymond is married and has two beautiful children, Isabel and Presley Fernandez. He loves history, especially when it pertains to growing up in La Mirada and running through the lakes within Neff Park during the rainy season. He enjoyed many fun memories at La Mirada High School with some unforgettable friends. He wants the readers to know especially of the youth and vibrancy of the city today and how we got here from a historical perspective. His hobbies include reading, writing, cooking, gardening and treasure hunting. He loves classical music and music from the 1940s thru the '80s, plays, poetry and great cinema. Most of all he loves time with family and sincere people.